The trademarks that are used are without any consent, and the publication of the trademark is without permission or backing by the trademark owner. All trademarks and brands within this book are for clarifying purposes only and are owned themselves, not affiliated with this document.

Table of Contents

Narcissistic Mothers

The Best Guide To Deal With Narcissistic Parenting. Learn The Best Abuse Recovery Techniques To Better Your Mother And Child Relationship And Never Suffer From Emotional Abuse

VIRGINIA FIX

Introduction

Being fiercely loyal and protective, mothers are the emotional backbone of their family. They protect their family's emotional needs and do everything they can to keep their children from being hurt. Everyone admires her. She balances with perfection being socially active while adding value to society to put others in reverence. She is the "Wonder woman" in their eyes. Most people don't know this "wonder woman" has a secret. She also has a flaw like everybody else in the world, as no one is perfect. No one is the paradigm of perfection in the mother's case, but narcissism is the issue.

Like other kids, a child of a narcissistic mother cannot demand more of her. Still, she may get annoyed for not doing homework, making a disorder, or accidentally irritating her.

When a child gets a little older, awareness develops, and he begins to observe that the mother lacks normal parenting behavior when he compares other kids and mother interaction.

Normal parents interact with their kids with ease, but a narcissistic parent only wants to conquer the argument. It is both miserable and terrifying. So a child grows up quietly and cautiously around a toxic mother, in the hope that's, she's in a nice mood, and beware of not inciting her anger. All it takes a little to be good.

Children who a narcissistic mother has raised may continue to experience emotional and mental tactics. A child learns that her actions are not uncontrolled. It is either a golden child or a scapegoat.

Chapter 1: A Hidden Demon

1.1 What is Narcissism?

The word "narcissist" is associated with people who are sure of themselves. There is also a rising sense of narcissism across the world, and most part of the psychological investigation does not confirm this notion.

Narcissism is a fundamental problem with identity or self. Narcissistic people are empty inside. They have few boundaries and very poor self-esteem. They may project confidence and grandiosity (a sense of power, success, and superiority), but these projections are just a defense against underlying feelings of worthlessness.

Narcissists have limited ability to see other people as separate or autonomous. They will normally consider everything in terms of how it relates to them. This makes it hard for them to see or accept differences of opinion and they often become filled with rage in response to disagreements or criticism. It can make life with a narcissist unpredictable and painful.

In 1898, Havelock Ellis (the British essayist and physician) was the first to identify Narcissism as a mental disorder. The disorder is based on a mythological role who loved his reflection. It is considered a normal stage in a child's development but is marked as a disorder during adolescence. People who display these traits are unable to keep positive self-esteem. They constantly try to get praise from others by pursuing others or forcing them to say positive things. Narcissism is considered to reflect a form of chronic interpersonal self-esteem regulation. Narcissism is much deeper and destructive, with devastating effects on the people living around them.

1.2 The Traits of Narcissism

Narcissism encompasses a desire for appreciation, a hunger for insecurity, and a perception of higher status. Research finds that they are more egocentric. An extreme narcissism can be damaging in every relationship.

How to distinguish a narcissist? Narcissists are also difficult to tell apart from ordinary people. Narcissism is difficult to detect by MRI or another medical testing. Therapists look for clues from the traits that people exhibit. Narcissism is distinguished by a sense of inflated self-worth, a lack of compassion, and a desire for constant admiration. They think that they are privileged and deserve special treatment. If you encounter someone who consistently exhibits these traits, you are dealing with a narcissistic individual. A person affected by this has an inflated sense of self-righteousness, a hang-up on fantasies of gaining, triumph, and authority.

The defining symptom of this is an overestimated vision of oneself that can be seen in different situations. The self-worth is greater than what is accomplished by the individual. Individuals with this disorder are typically selfish and cold-blooded to the needs and desires of others. They are likely to be seen as arrogant. The disorder is common in men and in adulthood.

Following are the distinguishing traits of a narcissist, but not all have these traits.

1.2.1 Above Others

The most important feature of a narcissist is self-importance. Self-confidence alone is not enough. Narcissists have a black/white view of the world. Narcissists are first, but others can still climb the ladder. Narcissists have to be the best, most right, and most competent.

Narcissists derive their superiority from being disrespected and disappointed. Covert narcissists expect to receive reassurance and have a right to hurt others to even things out (calm down).

1.2.2 Demand for Affection

Narcissists demand continuous care and love. Narcissistic authentication is considered if others say yes. Even if it does not count much, it is something important. For a selfish person, their need for acceptance is akin to a funnel. They should praise their mother and mother-in-law so that they feel happy.

Narcissists have deep-rooted insecurity that causes them to not believe anyone loves them. A narcissist is not a courageous, considerate or decisive person. They never really feel good about themselves.

1.2.3 Perfectionism

One can identify them due to their excessive need for perfection. They think things should be perfect, as they should, everything occurs precisely as they have imagined, and life should unfold as they planned. This is an oppressive requirement which makes the narcissist unhappy mostly. The demand for perfection motivates them to be dissatisfied and vocal about it.

1.2.4 Authority

To control everything is a narcissistic trademark trait. Narcissists are perpetually dissatisfied with the imperfect way life happens, and therefore they like to control life and bad things to make life favorable. They insist on having control, and their sense of belonging seems to them to be the "logical" thing to do.

They have a pre-conceived story in mind as to how their conversations should develop. When people don't follow their expected behavior, people become depressed and imbalanced. When things aren't going according to the planned script, they require verbalizing and acting according to their desired conclusion. People are a part of their internal dialogue; the play characters do not have their own emotions and thinking. (As can be stuck with a narcissist for too long).

1.2.5 Blame others

Narcissists do not feel responsible, the main issue with them. Narcissists like to control everything but want to let loose and not be held responsible if things go awry. If one met a narcissist and things don't go the way they planned out, the narcissist may place all the ills on others. That blame is made public because everyone is out to victimize him. The narcissist will blame others the most in the office, and they will be the source of their misery. As they like to be superior- with no errors, they accuse others of mess. Blaming means that people will have more trust and sympathy.

1.2.6 No walls

People crossing each other's boundaries are common among narcissists. Narcissists do not understand where their ideas end and theirs begin. They're both very immature, two-year-old. These people all believe everything told, they all think the same, and they all want the same things. These people are most insulted to hear that "No" It won't take much effort for a narcissist to get what he or she wants. These are classic narcissistic behavior

1.2.7 No emotions

They lack sympathy, one of the hallmark characteristics of a narcissist. They are egocentric and lack compassion for others. They assume that everyone acts and thinks just like them and often give any clue of their feelings. They are stubborn, aggressive, and hardly apologetic.

Some narcissists may not know what emotions are and how they work. They don't know how they feel. They believe their emotions are the result of outside forces. They overlook the role of their biology in their thoughts and emotions. Therefore, narcissists blame others for their negative feelings. They claim people failed to accomplish their desires or that their actions hurt their emotions.

No sympathy makes genuine bonds with them difficult or impossible. They don't care what others are thinking.

1.2.8 Fear threat

People with narcissistic tendencies are very alert to dangers, rage, and no from people but frequently misinterpret body language as hostile. If one is emulating selfish behavior, the narcissist will not accurately interpret their emotions. Even saying "I apologize" in response to the narcissist's anger can exacerbate the situation. They may not trust and misinterpret what others are saying.

Additionally, if they don't carefully choose what to say, they will reply incorrectly or become defensive. They perceive sarcasm as an agreement, and they misinterpret jovial banter between friends as an attack when it isn't. The lack of ability to read expressions, a common narcissistic trait, is enough to make narcissists deficiently empathetic towards others. They don't perceive an emotion that doesn't exist, they don't understand their point, and they think others feel the same as they do.

1.2.9 Sentimental rationale

Trying to rationalize and reason with them does not work. Others believe that if people accept responsibility for their actions, they will change. Explanation of people is irrelevant to the narcissist, who only seems capable of recognizing emotions and desires from their own perspective. Narcissists may claim to understand but do not actually understand.

Narcissists make their decisions after considering only how they perceive anything. If consumers want a red sports car, they will purchase a red sports car no matter its real cost. This is what happens if people want to try something different. They look to someone outside to meet their needs. They like that others go with their plans and they feel attacked if others don't.

1.2.10 Splitting

Narcissists have a split personality because they consider themselves good or bad. Criticism or negativity is perceived as personal shortcomings, which they put on the victim. They continuously accuse others of their pessimistic approach. They view things with their eyes. They can't seem to impose sanctions on them.

Narcissists cannot accurately perceive the positive or negative aspects of a happening. Narcissists cannot handle more than one perspective simultaneously.

1.2.11 Zero tolerance to NO

The life of a narcissist is led by fear. A narcissist would have a deep-seated irrational fear of being criticized. They concern about germs, money, being attacked, being seen as bad, being abandoned, or being an object of ridicule. This makes it difficult to trust others; therefore, it makes it difficult to work with others.

Relationships become closer, the less trustworthy they will be. Narcissists fear true affection or being available because they are afraid others will judge them because of their negative qualities. The encouragement has no impact on the narcissist because he/she dislikes herself so much. Narcissists cannot ever develop a trust for other people to love them, and they constantly try to test others to find the line of love. The feeling of not being noticed or rejected will never subside.

1.2.12 Depression

Sadness is constantly felt. Some people who have low self-esteem show sadness by talking excessively about the impending doom that is certain to happen and also lessen their sadness. Narcissists feel threatened by their loved ones, and this is reflected in the relationship. This is all designed to avoid anxiety in a loved one so that they won't feel any hardship. As he feels sad, she feels good. The individuals feel stronger because of feeling sadness and stress.

1.2.13 Shame

They only feel a small amount of shame because they believe they are right, and they believe their behaviors do not really affect others. At times, they do harbor a lot of guilt. In the heart of the narcissist are all the ones buried beneath oppressive repression. He is ashamed of his self-destructive thoughts and feelings. Narcissists must avoid revealing their weaknesses to others to keep up themselves. They cannot act real or be genuine to others.

1.2.14 An inability to be truly vulnerable

This reason alone is why narcissists are unable to love and connect well with people. They cannot see the world the way we see it. This makes them very insecure. If a relationship is not fulfilling, people tend to link up with another partner whenever possible. They desire someone who will sympathize with their pain and would make things as they want them to be. It's interdependency, except they offer a little help to their partners.

1.2.15 An inability to articulate

The reflective, mutually cooperative behaviors involve a well-defined awareness of each person's emotions. How will this person feel? How will this affect our communication? These are subjects that narcissists are incapable of realizing. People should not be expecting the narcissist to recognize their feeling or give in to what they want. It is ineffective.

1.3 Kinds of Narcissism

Though narcissistic personality disorder is recognized, there exists no diagnosis for traits such as narcissism. Some forms of narcissism have been identified, and the validity of such an idea has been confirmed through peer-reviewed research. Therefore, there is no concrete number of narcissistic personality subtypes.

The Following are the types:

1.3.1. Good Health Narcissism

Healthy narcissism does also exist. Many people may possess certain narcissistic traits without being diagnosed as having NPD. This is a separate category with its own positive aspect, that is, narcissism.

A person with healthy narcissistic tendencies will feel good about his/her achievements and want to share those achievements with others because they make him/her feel good. This is also the ability to be presumptuous and perceive oneself as having an entitlement mentality. These feelings appear in many people's lives.

1.3.2. Grandiose narcissism

The closest synonym to grandiose narcissism is "arrogant and self-absorbed." It pertains to overly high self-esteem. Grandiose narcissism involves overestimating one's abilities, asserting one's dominance over others, and having a generally inflated sense of self-esteem.

This kind has been tested and proven empirically, but other kinds are shown to be healthy (also known as covert narcissism).

This is when a person with high narcissistic tendencies shows their characteristics openly at the cost of others. Narcissistic people can be charismatic but fall short of empathic. They are not used to relate to other humans but rather to impress them. They may be attracted to people who are angry, weak, or confused.

In dealing with them or a narcissist in general, setting boundaries is vital. Be aware we can convey grace and assertiveness simultaneously. They will push limits to the point of irrelevancy in order to secure a steady stream of business. Be prepared to enforce their personal boundaries, and ideally, walk away.

1.3.3. Vulnerable narcissism, also known as covert narcissism

This is also referred to as vulnerable narcissism. On the contrary, these people are reserved and non-aggressive. People who have a reputation to maintain often get very protective whenever their reputation is called into question.

1.3.4. Insidious narcissism

They are quite malicious. Narcissistic personality disorder (NPD) is characterized by a lack of empathy and selfishness.

The malignant narcissist gets pleasure in inflicting stress and depression. So it is recommended to avoid them as much as possible and sever all ties.

1.3.5. Sexual narcissism

They are unreliable partners, can use sex to exploit others, and are often aggressive while having sex. One way to avoid narcissistic abuse is to terminate the association and to seek counseling from a specialist.

This is a three-tier system of narcissism, including somatic narcissism and cerebral narcissism. The major downside is that no one has been researched, nor are they validated by research.

1.3.6. Somatic narcissism

They tend to care excessively about their physical appearance and raise an objection against others based on their looks. They often disregard the concerns of others to focus on their own needs. One shouldn't get involved in any drama concerning their narcissist.

1.3.7. Cerebral narcissist

The cerebral narcissist derives his significance from his intellect compared to the somatic narcissist, who derives meaning from his physique.

Narcissists regard themselves as superior to other humans. They will desperately try to make us feel insignificant and invalid. If dealing with a narcissist, we must be certain.

1.3.8. Spiritual narcissist

Narcissists use spirituality to belittle and victimize others. The narcissist needs an idealized version of himself to avoid his deep-seated identity conflict, and spiritual narcissists use seemingly sensitive actions as a way to be above others.

People who have experienced a lot of upheavals are at greater risk of being victims of spiritual narcissists' "charming, stimulating influence."

1.4 Narcissistic Abuses Employed

So why are narcissists involved in emotionally manipulative conduct, in particular? Normally, they have "narcissistic injuries" or feel the urge to manipulate someone.

Narcissists have an over-exaggerated grandiose perception of themselves, and the narcissist wants the universe and, in particular, its companion to support the view. If other people challenge or disturb the view, the narcissist encounters a so-called narcissistic injury. More simply, the narcissist sees a danger to himself as fine, sane, kind, omnipotent, and essential, worthy of special care, and so on. Narcissistic damage may occur very often when a narcissist's opinion is out of sync with the facts.

After a narcissist encounters a narcissistic accident, he or she generally becomes protective and sometimes angry. This is termed "narcissistic rage." If someone remarks that the narcissist finds a challenge or insult, the narcissist devalues the person who made the statement by verbal harassment to lose respect in the eyes of the narcissist. This helps him to retain his unrealistic expectations of himself.

The narcissistic anger may take the form of emotional or physical violence is significant. Persons with a narcissistic personality disorder will readily switch from verbal assault to physical abuse. If the target of verbal and emotional violence becomes more conscious (or more serious) of abuse, it would be best to quit until physical abuse rises.

Narcissistic violence can often start when the attacker may regain care over others. He or she will achieve that by insulting the victims and having them feel psychologically and morally incompetent. For example, a narcissist might convince his victims again and again that they are useless or insulted in public. The narcissist assumes that the survivor would slip deeper under his influence, withholding his consent in order to finally gain recognition. Sadly, this is also the case.

Abuse Forms

It is crucial to note that physical violence may start as mild (pinching, pushing) but would more certainly intensify when the survivor doesn't quit the narcissistic offender. Emotional and verbal harassment may be almost as harmful as physical abuse, if not worse. The consequences of verbal, emotional, or physical violence may be long-term and debilitating. All the acts of a survivor of an emotionally and verbally manipulative narcissist are as follows:

1. Carelessness – retention of passion, friendship, sensitivity, and familiarity.
2. Countering – Where the partner reflects, and the attacker automatically counters his opinion without reacting to it or taking it into consideration.
3. Discounts – Where the offender relieves the opinions or feelings of his spouse, advising the partner that his suggestions are meaningless, wrong, or dumb. The attacker also limits the memory of the partner about the violence itself.
4. Verbal violence dressed as witches – these "jokes," particularly if delivered openly, maybe quite hurtful.
5. Blocking and diversion – The attacker switches the topic as the partner tries to address an issue and avoids a future conversation or resolution.
6. Accusation and accusation – The attacker suspects, the partner of a felony. The offender may be conscious that the spouse is innocent of

the suspected wrongdoing, but this strategy serves the function of protecting the partner instead of analyzing the abuser's actions.

7. Narcissists are believed to use a projection" to project their own bad actions or emotions on the survivor, accusing the victim of what the offender did or feels.
8. Judging and accusing – This weakens the self-esteem of the partner and creates the need for the survivor to search for the attacker.
9. Trivialization – This is where the offender minimizes something that is significant for the girlfriend, for example, fear regarding the abuser.
10. Undermining – The attacker feels intimidated and attempts to deter his wife if the partner decides to do something better about him/her. It may be an open order, indirectly convincing the partner that it's a poor idea or a secret move that will discourage the partner from traveling.
11. Threats – Threats of a breakup, leaving, harassment or any threats that (psychologically or physically) harm the spouse or someone who loves.
12. Calling the name - This dehumanizes the spouse/victim and erodes the self-esteem of the partner.
13. Oblivion – sometimes the offender 'forgets' instances of violence that damage the truth of the partner. The offender will even "forget" items which his or her wife knows are really significant.
14. Orders – treating the companion as an infant or a slave; ignoring the partner's freedom.
15. Denial – the attacker disputes his/her behavior constantly. This lowers a partner's truth (this is often called "crazy-making").
16. Abusive wrath – Anytime the attacker becomes angry to frighten the girlfriend. This anger is also triggered by events that are unimportant for a non-abuser.

The victim's physical or psychiatric decline is an indication that they need support. For victims of narcissistic violence, there is a significant healing process; it starts with self-education. The survivor and the attacker should pursue independent care since each procedure is different. The companion should continue with being better educated about the narcissistic personality dysfunction (NPD), which afflicts the narcissistic abuser, to recognize that it is not their responsibility, considering what the abuser has assured them over and over. They are victims. They are victims. For victims of narcissistic bullying as well as individual treatment, there are several recovery groups.

The abundance of resources and education about substance addiction is a valuable starting point because it lets the addict recover power over their own lives. The social groups help the abused to connect with those who experience similar traumas and may alleviate the burden of being alone desperately. Therefore, NPD patients may obtain advice to recognize their condition and assess the root conditions that drive the illness.

1.5 How Does Someone Become Narcissistic?

There is research that suggests that parenting styles and genetic factors may be contributing factors in the development of narcissism. Certain parenting styles seem to have an inverse effect on those who already have a biological predisposition to be narcissistic. The permissive or authoritarian parenting styles can lead to greater interpersonal problems, such as unhealthy narcissism.

Indulgent parenting style

Children are in danger when parents or caregivers show excessive praise and a lack of limits. Children hear they have special talents or receive little criticism, so they believe they are gifted, special, and so on. Some parents praise their children in a different way on occasion (rewarding a child with a huge gift when he cleans up his room, for example). This could lead to narcissism because a child could feel entitled or grandiose.

Authoritative parenting

A lack of empathy or lack of love makes a child very frustrated. In some instances, parents do not know when they should show empathy. It can cause a person to become psychologically unhealthy, which eventually causes them to exploit others.

Aggressive parenting

This parenting style is demonstrated as healthy and effective. Parents play important roles: one parent can make up for the shortcomings of the other. Showing love and being empathic and responsive to children will help them internalize these factors.

Traumatic experiences

Experiencing traumatic events can help the development of certain narcissistic traits. Those who deal with traumatic experiences develop certain narcissistic tendencies, which can eventually result in NPD. The major themes in this study involved the loss of a positive caregiver, severe neglect, and bullying. Traumatic experiences can cause trust issues to develop. A lot of narcissists are suspicious and wary of others.

1.6 How narcissism is treated?

Treatment for narcissism can be difficult, but therapy may cure this.

Therapy Types:

- Considerate psychotherapy that uses behavioral techniques both psychodynamic and emotional, frequently coupled with psychopharmacologic management.
- Constructed psychotherapy processes.
- Mentalization-based care.
- Clients are able to rely on themselves,
- Psychotherapy that emphasizes transference.
- Identifies the therapeutic objective of the patient and developed a counseling arrangement between the psychiatrist and the patient.
- Schema-concentrated psychotherapy.
- Cognitive-behavioral counseling, attachment theory, and psychodynamic therapy are used to treat negative views of one's, others, and one's status in the world that are created in a young life.
- Behavioral, dialectical treatment.
- There are key principles of understanding and progress in cognitive-behavioral therapy (CBT) that incorporate individual therapy with group treatment.

Medications are also used to treat Narcissistic Personality Disorder (NPD), especially in patients with serious symptoms that may be a risk to themselves or anyone, and in patients with other health issues that may be hard to treat.

Medications for the treatment of narcissistic personality disorder include the following:

1. Stabilizers in mood
2. Antipsychotics
3. Antidepressants

1.7 When Narcissism Is A Disorder Not A Trait

Self-absorption is a common trait among adolescent males. However, most teens usually grow out of this total self-absorption and an ability to care about others. In terms of narcissistic traits that continue into adulthood is how people see nothing wrong with themselves and believe that everyone needs to change their way of thinking. When people are like that, they can make people angry.

We all have some type of traits or personalities, which some people think are psychopathic or sociopathic. One develops narcissism from early childhood.

1.8 Difference between Narcissism and Narcissistic Personality Disorder

All narcissistic personality disorder people are narcissistic, but all narcissistic are not NPD. There is a fine line between them. Narcissistic Disorder (NPD) is defined by an inflated sense of self-importance and grandiosity. These people often lose friends and family due to their self-obsession and grandiosity but can replace them quickly.

People with NPD have mood swings. The cruel behavior is contradictory and leaves the victim often confused and anxious.

Narcissists not having the disorder; these individuals are selfish or desire admiration due to loss of care, which was rooted in their childhood.

People, narcissists and those having disorders can improve the damage through therapy and proper consultation. But mostly, they do not accept the fact that they are mentally healthy.

The term "narcissist" means someone who is excessively self-centered, who makes every conversation about themselves, and who takes mean decisions over others' welfare. Other people are not aware of an exaggerated sense of self characterizes a debilitating condition. The disorder is called narcissistic personality disorder (NPD). This paper seeks to differentiate between narcissism and being a narcissist. Let us first review the definition of narcissistic personality disorder and then the intricacies of narcissism as a personality trait.

Narcissistic Personality Disorder (NPD)

Narcissistic Personality Disorder (NPD) is an illness characterized by exaggerated self-estimation. Many people with narcissistic personality disorder fail to recognize that they have a narcissistic personality disorder, and they fail to seek counseling. They suffer the social consequences of their friends and family members losing contact with them, but they are adept at finding new friends and partners. When they get older, they become difficult to live with; their self-centered nature wears everyone to the bone. They prefer to live alone and prefer to be left alone when they're older. These very things they do to keep people attached are what will make people want to move on. The two behaviors are explained as follows:

- **They utilize intermittent reinforcement:** These individuals are unpredictable at best. They are loving, and then they are hateful. They love to bomb and then withhold favors. What they do is a gradual process that is highly undetectable initially. This method to eradicate the bad habit may take time. They leave their targets in a state of constant doubt and fear. It's like emotional gambling to be hooked on to some person.

- **They target codependents:** Individuals with Narcissistic Personality Disorder target codependent people as well as people who consider themselves too nice to others. Flattery, charm, and all types of tricks will be used to trick them into working for their schemes. Narcissistic Personality Disorder will make them become predatory. This disorder occurs in the same cluster of disorders as histrionic, antisocial, and borderline personality. They lack feelings.

While NPD's initial symptoms are devastating, we as a society know that this illness can be managed very well. The most common types of treatment are counseling and therapy.

Narcissism as a Personality Trait

Narcissism is a part of human personality. They are given the full name Narcissistic Personality Disorder. A narcissistic person is sometimes selfish in one part of their life, but they are not disturbed. Another example of vanity is someone who is constantly ruminating about their appearance. This is possible NPD. Confidence in school may be the issue at hand.

Narcissists also have a lot of empathy towards their loved ones. They are likely to have this quality in other areas of their lives. They don't damage or mistreat others. They don't have to be a narcissist in all areas. People with healthy narcissism have the skills to accomplish their goals. But if that person walks over and causes damage or injury to someone else, they will be mentally disturbed.

Living with NPD or Narcissistic Tendencies

Narcissistic tendencies aren't as dangerous as NPD. Indeed, though, people with narcissism and narcissistic personality disorder can find help. There is a curative therapy for NPD. Therapy often helps individuals with NPD deal with situations in their lives and become more successful. Even those who do not suffer from a personality disorder can be happier if they realize their condition and change their behavior.

1.9 Fixing NPD

The strongest method of therapy for narcissism is discovering how not to be narcissistic.

Many people claim it is possible to alter the narcissist's actions.

The query was, "Is there a cure for people with narcissistic tendencies?" was mixed with "IS there a cure for a narcissist?" They both differ a lot.

The first answer is NO for the first question and YES for the second question, whilst the second answer could be YES for the first question and NO for the second question.

In regards to the first one

There are no clinical experiments (studies) for NPD, BPD, etc., for any medication. (Narcissistic Personality Disorder and its Relation to Borderline Personality Disorder). It can be cured through talk therapy, as it is caused by genetic inheritance, how a child was raised, or a combination of both. If NPD has narcissistic traits, they can be cured through talk therapy.

About the second, a narcissistic individual has the capacity to change as the person is not a narcissist. Thus, identifying words regarding narcissism and allowing others to understand more about the subject is a question. "Narcissist" is someone that has a narcissistic personality disorder, while a narcissistic individual wouldn't actually have a narcissistic personality disorder. So, what are the differences?

Somebody who has NPD may have problems with places such as:

- Splitting.

- No stable relationship.

- Lack of emotions.

- Lack of guilt for oneself.

- These factors together affect the way narcissists perceive truth, which is somewhat different for others.

They would not be able to realize why someone really respects them. If one is mad with a narcissist, they cannot understand that they are really valued. They consider it in terms of absolute principles. People are either "all good" or "all bad." No opinion takes into consideration both sides for everyone.

This leads narcissists to still desire to be treated as the "all good" in a scenario. The smallest type of error is not appropriate. The consequence of an acute susceptibility to others' perceptions about oneself will significantly affect one's day-to-day relationships with others and contribute to serious self-esteem concerns and a conflicted view of his or her true worth.

An individual may have narcissism, but with therapy, to make their narcissism properly pass as usual. It is definitely the case that young people establish a kind of selfish self-absorption, but as they grow up, they become less so. Especially caring for children is a significant element in relationships—it goes a long way toward helping many people develop out of narcissism and help get them involved in an engagement in protecting their relationships with the people they value.

There are several obstacles people face, some of which contribute to a positive effect and others that drive one negatively. Any people who go through a life-altering illness or injury are now at the bottom of the social ladder and are trying to gain wealth and prosperity for themselves. Some catastrophic events have a net beneficial impact on people's attitudes by exposing them facets of their personalities they have not historically known, which causes them to adjust their mindset to the effect that they are able to assume more personal accountability for their behavior.

Narcissist persons do get well, but Narcissistic not.

1.10 Who is a Narcissistic Parent?

We ought to think of our parents as fine in our early lives. We will slowly embrace a more realistic image as we grow. Parents who are narcissistic will eventually have their children traumatized. They exploit them and manipulate them psychologically and use them to satisfy their own desires. Usually, these interactions are far too difficult for young minds to adopt.

Narcissistic parents are people who are overly concerned about themselves and, in some cases, believe that their children only exist to meet their needs, desires, and demands. This thinking can cause emotional harm to children in the long run. A narcissistic parent lacks the tenderness to care for and honor the child's dignity, well-being, and personality that a child requires for their adequate emotional and mental development.

1.11 Types of Narcissistic Parents

Engulfing

The engulfing narcissistic parent is too involved in a child's life, often exerting too much control and having no consideration for a child's boundaries. They regard children as a shared extension with no individual identity of their own. They try to mold a child into being what they want rather than considering what a child needs and wants.

Ignoring

The ignoring narcissistic parent will usually ignore a child whenever a child tries to make contact. Ignore oneself, feelings, and accomplishments, and are very apathetic towards issues pertaining to life. They don't do things for them because they consider kids unimportant to them. Furthermore, people will want recognition for everything they do, regardless of how insignificant.

1.12 Signs That One May Have a Narcissistic Parent

Narcissistic parents have specific movements, acts, and words. Self-soothing, self-promotion, and self-indulgence are learned behaviors. They also need support from their parents. So, children need parents for physical, mental, and emotional development. Some narcissists become parents to have a child as a form of dependence. Narcissists may devalue a child or transform a child into an extension of them. The following signs reveal that one may have a narcissistic parent.

1.12.1. Selfish

A narcissistic parent will momentarily praise kids but ultimately will continue to focus on their own achievements. It has to include them. They want to be the center of attention and will take risks or exaggerate claims in order to attract attention. They rarely listen to a child and are often unavailable for any interactions. They believe the world revolves around them.

1.12.2. Lack of Empathy

A narcissistic parent values their own ego and feelings above all else. They don't seem to put any effort into understanding what a child is going through, and they never ask how a child is doing.

1.12.3. Dependency Issues

Whether it is emotionally, physically, or financially, narcissistic parents will expect that children take care of them regardless of their age and/or actual needs. They will nudge children into behaving in ways that they would not otherwise choose to do. They prioritize their needs over a child but demand that child is completely available. Their independence prompts them to object. They will get upset if a child has not called and spoken with them in a while.

Some narcissistic parents may also enable their adult children to engage in irresponsible behavior by giving them material gifts. To illustrate, it will enable them to continue a drug or alcohol habit or prevent them from being successful in anything on their own. This way, they remain dependent on them, and they are held back from creating a truly independent life. Because narcissistic parents often hope that their child will live under their influence forever, they may become extremely jealous of any signs of their growing independence and maturity.

1.12.4. Blame game

They will manipulative to make a child feels like he owes them something when, in reality, he didn't. They will use guilt-tripping tactics to manipulate and then blame a child for their shortcoming. They also play the victim card and shift blame to children for all the mess.

1.12.5. Emotional Blackmailing

Narcissistic parents will punish a child if he does anything wrong in their eyes, but actually, a child did not. They play emotional tactics to let him feel unworthy. Children become emotionally weak to survive difficult phases of life.

1.12.6. Ignore Limits

They usually ignore a child's personal space and will not be ashamed of crossing the limits as they consider this right to do so. They never let their child come out of egg-shell.

1.12.7. Gaslight

It is an exploitative technique to have authority over a child. Lies, ignorance, and squeezing are employed to make a child crazy. They will even consider themselves victim and put the blame on a child for the mess they created. They create a web of fraud and drama. Gas lighting is an often verbally manipulative and tyrannical technique that can be very successful as a power play. The illusion will eventually get stronger and lead the victim to conclude they may be insane. It can impair mental health, resulting in distrust of people in general, which can interfere with establishing stable relationships in the future.

Adult children of abusive parents often expend a long time attempting to question their nurturing responsibility during the early stages of life. For a narcissist, this almost never goes well. It is not my definition of a nice time. It is common for authoritarian parents to reject the truth, call their children liars, or simply say they don't recall things that way at all (i.e., their child may have been mistaken). As the adult child is abandoned, he or she feels more pain, disappointment, and angst. They do something in order to be justified or accepted. Also, it leaves them with one more impression of something that wasn't theirs or that they couldn't manage, and they come away from it again feeling loss and a sense of authenticity.

1.12.8. Demand a child to behave as Parent

They don't act as a parent should, and they often expect their children to take on the responsibilities they should be doing. This includes caring for them, reaching out to them, and discussing their health. They are overly demanding and insist upon getting too much from them but offer little in return – little emotional support, advice, and encouragement. But in their eyes, they perceive themselves as being generous and beneficent. They wish to be praised for their warped worldview. As they say, it's their world; they make the rules.

1.12.9. Always Right

Try talking to narcissistic parents about their bad behavior, and they will turn the conversation into a HUGE argument. They will overreact, admit no faults, and deny everything. Ultimately, they will be put in a bad situation. The cycle of violence never stops, no matter how hard it's worked on. Even if a child would like to have a heart-to-heart exchange, they will not try to hear. For them, it is never the fault of the victim, but always that person or another who is to blame.

1.12.10. Stubbornness

A narcissistic parent likely won't change his or her behavior. People who act this way do not like being pointed out or accused of irrationality. They are sensitive because they want to control children. They love when a child follows what they want or prove he is "worthy" to them. They will quickly withdraw love if he does not meet their needs. The narcissist reacts negatively when they realize they cannot always manipulate him.

1.12.11. Lame Excuses

They always want attention because they are attention-seekers. They care only about themselves and feel sorry for themselves, yet do nothing to better their lives. Thus, make lame excuses to get rid of any responsibility that comes in their way, to achieve satisfaction by ignoring the child's needs.

1.12.12. Like to insult

Narcissistic parents insult because they also like to boost their own grandeur. They demean the child, rejecting positive attitudes or emotions. They may even put down a child's skills. They like to monopolize the conversation with children, even yelling at them, which they think is right to do to make children walk on their way or follow the highway. This notion insults the dignity and integrity of a child.

1.13 Children Raised By a Narcissistic Mother or Father

Their child has trust issues, anxiety or depression, as well as difficulties dealing with and expressing emotions. A child constantly struggles to make others happy and seeks validation every time they make a decision. Do not have a strong sense of themselves, want, need, or goal. Exaggerate their accomplishments to gain a feeling of self-esteem. They suffer emptiness, toxic shame, self-hatred, becoming people-pleaser, low self-love, lack of personal limits, and dependency issues. A very critical consideration for manipulative adult children is that they do not understand that narcissists are one or both of their parents! They may usually recognize that their upbringing was incorrect or that their parents were off in any manner, but with whom they were or are, they do not actually acknowledge their parents.

This leaves them at a great disadvantage, and they will have tremendous problems with their life without understanding why before they grasp narcissism and mind control. In spite of their successes, challenges such as feeling inferior to some, compromising their desires to help others, and sometimes feeling bad as adults for disobeying their parents, often sometimes long after the parents are gone! Adult offspring of narcissists will have certain thoughts and convictions that are so profoundly rooted that they cannot really contemplate challenging certain items until they purposely reverse the manipulation endured by their parents' hands.

The effects of being raised by a narcissistic mother or father are as follows:

1.13.1.   Poor self-esteem

Children of narcissists are constantly on the receiving end of being shamed. As a direct consequence of their overanxious parents, a child believes like they are never good enough. And as narcissists, the parents seek excellence out of their children, and they are unable to receive it. These feelings of low-esteem may work their way through a child's adulthood and affect their mental wellbeing.

1.13.2.   Isolation

If their self-esteem is poor (because their parents are low), certain children of narcissists become so terrified of failing that they also become scared of attempting. They make them feel awkward by isolating themselves from resources, others because they feel left out. Instead, they might have a manipulative adult who doesn't encourage a child to be confident in becoming relaxed with them. This pushes a child to feel vulnerable and off the beaten track.

1.13.3.   Issues relating to abandonment

Narcissists do not offer any validation to their offspring. It is really unusual that individuals have children with this condition, so their children don't know how to manage it when they do. For certain instances, an infant stays confident so often that the same child is overbearing to others. Adulthood is a period of tremendous development during which certain individuals have difficulties sustaining stable relationships with others.

1.13.4.   The experience of becoming self-conscious

Narcissists educate their offspring with a sharp eye wherever they want, often in desirable conditions. When mothers with small children are often too much mocked by their mates, it safe to proceed because they do not notice their children too much. As adults, their children become rather self-conscious about having the views of others, and also the opinions of their children, the way they look, and their attempts to appear friendly to their children's mates. People who were appreciated sufficiently as adolescents seldom send out constructive signals to the world as adults.

1.13.5.   A type of inferiority complex

Parents who have selfish traits equate their children to other children. As a consequence, these children felt like they are not successful enough as a result.

In other terms, they grow up with a loss of self-esteem.

1.13.6.   Depression and fear overcome

Low self-esteem and the subsequent failure to cope with abandonment and feelings of inadequacy may contribute to depression. These features often alienate and preclude anyone from establishing and sustaining a positive friendship between themselves and other people. It is to be an attempt to learn how to respect themselves. Even as an infant, having tendencies toward anxiety and depression may grow. When they grow older, teenagers become more responsible.

1.13.7.   Being afraid to speak out

Narcissistic parents also pressure their children to hold their views to themselves or not have opinions at all. Owing to this, it is because a child grows up with an unwillingness to express their own thoughts.

1.13.8.   The individual self-destructs

When a child is raised with a narcissistic parent, it transforms a child into a telenovela, which is a circumstance of an unhealthy and destructive atmosphere. They unwittingly gravitate towards or establish dysfunctional partnership dynamics and circumstances. When they experience healthier partnerships, they sometimes self-sabotage them and fake emotional triggers to go back to the dysfunctional, abusive relationships; they believe they just do not give up.

1.13.9.   This person is really responsive

A kid who was treated by a narcissist is hypersensitive to anything they don't really want to perceive. This is the only emotional speech a child has to do for life since it shows how to respond to parents' mood changes. Grownups in those years become cautious around other people's emotions.

1.13.10. The lack of limits

Narcissists' offspring inherit the most dangerous stuff from their parents. The most toxic of these is their utter failure to place rules for themselves. Since they are readily distinguished, it is convenient for individuals to misuse or manipulate them during the workplace. They really want things to go smoothly, which ensures they constantly are able to risk too much of themselves to give people the recognition they deserve. Even the slightest errors at work and in relationships will lead an individual to beat themselves up. This is why they can't find out how to work hard with their profession or how to contribute to their peers.

1.13.11. Being codependent

Since the narcissistic parent lacked self-worth, there is a loss of self-esteem and a strong sense of self inside their infant. This is significant since children learn how to develop a healthier relationship through their parents.

The stress that children endured as an infant and their parents' co-dependence has enabled them to have a distorted perspective of their adult relationships.

1.13.12. A poor sense of self

It is necessary to retain a good sense of self, day in and day out. It keeps the consumer from contrasting oneself to others. Having this, we can realize we can pull it off. Most notably, the student establishes a clear personality.

If an adult child decides to stick near with a manipulative parent, this could defeat the adult child's own aspirations to build an identity. Because of this, they constantly inquire about whom they are or what they desire.

1.13.13. Feeling continually guilty/ashamed

The effect in all of this is internalized toxic guilt, which is based around the notion that in true self is unlovable. The worst yet most normal "feeling" that a person may experience is feeling unworthy or self-conscious. This disease will grow worse and is finally crippling.

1.13.14. There is a sense of rivalry

This over-competitiveness tends to surface when a parent has unrealistic aspirations for their infant. Often that is a positive idea, but sometimes it isn't. Being competitive at the job means employees are good.

1.14 Children Dynamics in Narcissistic Family

If there are more than two children living in a household, narcissistic mothers can allocate each of them a separate and unique role. In the same family, there may only be one child who is preferred; however, responsibilities may be reversed or reassigned at the parent's will. If the family only has one child, a child may have to perform many tasks.

Following are the main positions assigned to children in a narcissistic family: "golden child," "scapegoat," and "lost/invisible child."

The Golden Child

Initially, one child is given the role of a golden child. He is the parent's "chosen one." The golden child is seen as an extension of his toxic parents. They live vicariously through him.

This infant reflects the mother's picture of her ideal self. He is either naturally desirable or has an ability that his parents think is very incredible. This child has been picked to be exploited for benefit.

He is never to be criticized. If the parents find fault in their children's actions, so something may be wrong with them. They elevate the very best specimen to a greater degree of omnipotence. They worship this guy as though he was a deity. Unlike strong, omnipotent gods or goddesses who do whatever they wish, this infant belongs to its mother.

The jealous parent wants to connect with the golden kid like they were one. This makes it really challenging for children to develop their own identities.

The demands put on the golden child were incredibly large. One of his key duties as a father is to make his or her parent look fine. His major obligation is to make his family satisfied.

f the golden boy is not up to speed with his responsibility, the parent brings him to the task. Though he is fearful for his position as scapegoat boy, a child hastily reverts into his assigned role.

He discovers that being easy to please, being really well-looking, and possessing charisma is what make him lovable. His condition will haunt him during his lifespan.

The Scapegoat Boy

The life of the scapegoat kid could be somewhat different. When there is a golden boy, there will still be a scapegoat that will "pay" for it. In certain households, there is more than one scapegoat child, and in some situations, the scapegoat is typically the perfect child, the "good" kid.

The parents regard a scapegoat infant as a "toxic person" that is as inferior as someone may be. Her life's primary aim is to bear the abusive parent's cause and legacies on her back. The family members fault everything that goes wrong in the family on him.

The parent who is narcissistic of this child is unrelenting in its judgment, malicious, and violent. Family members, most especially mum, aunts, and other relatives, refuse to respect him, making him feel ashamed and betrayed by his own family.

The scapegoat kid is the one in the family who is the most genuine, sincere, and sacrificing participant. Hence, it is still being handled unfairly. And in a case where he is exploited and used, he will always remember her importance and motivation source.

When a selfish adult uses an infant as a scapegoat, he sees a child as having no desires of his own, even if that adult wants to care about him. His whole life was spent attempting to measure up to the demands of his or her peers. That's not a smart plan every time. With no initiative on his side, he never reaches society's acceptance expectations.

Since he is branded a troublemaker for doing constructive stuff or negative acts, he is at a bit of a loose end thread. This kid needs special care. And if bad or optimistic, this also counts as "attention."

Finding admiration and carrying a grudge onto the other sibling, the scapegoat kid is adamant in disliking and criticizing the other sibling. He still struggles in his attempts. His output is judged to be subpar, lazy, or contradictory. The scapegoat girl truly lives out the self-destructive labels, and the defining mentality follows her throughout her life.

The scapegoat child had more independence than the golden child in their youth, but in that way, they do a bit better in adulthood. Since her lack of enmeshment with her father places her in a more sensitive and discrete role, she is more apt to get away from him and establish a sense of self. This is the irony of psychiatric disease, namely that it would lead her to lose a healthy sense of self. She would still feel like a lonely loser, even deep down inside.

The invisible/lost boy

The kid who is an unseen or lost part of the family is neither celebrated nor punished. This boy cannot be viewed in a manner as though he did not live. This person is invisible to everyone, unacknowledged by many, and sometimes overlooked. In relation to a teenager, a selfish adult may become totally oblivious and uninvolved in their desires. This girl obviously does nothing for this man.

The fundamentals of what's called "the invisible child" are sometimes forgotten over time. If he's sent to school in old and rusty clothing, he may become humiliated and ashamed. Often, his hair can be lank. The parent could, for whatever cause, not teach him proper hygiene. If he may not get sufficient medical attention, he will die. Parents who are selfish are willing to perceive that they may not get adequate attention, thus making sure that they may not reveal this fact to anyone.

As is the case for the unseen boy, the son is handled as though he is a "no one." He has no hopes and does not ask for anything. He is the calmest brother in the house, and no one pays much mind to him anyways. The golden child chooses to go his path without inclining or speaking to others, whilst the scapegoat child cleverly lifts his voice toward the father, but the parent even less notices the silent child's voice.

This child withdraws from himself, isolates, to shield himself from hurt. When he withdraws into himself, he appears to hide from the universe, into his own secluded place. He misses out on safe interpersonal experiences, such as an outing or a date. His friendships are typically limited if any. He just seems as though he blends in with certain groups of citizens.

These "ghosts" are very private to themselves, which can be impossible for some to grasp. Sometimes, individuals who are struggling with this condition lack a positive sense of connectedness to others. Having no one to depend on except oneself also contributes to depression and social isolation; however, they can generally stay self-sufficient.

He has never felt valued as a small boy, would waste his life becoming unseen, unlovable, and unworthy. This condition is vulnerable to including extreme distress among both the silent struggle kids and the other problems that arise with drug misuse as well as eating disorders.

Narcissistic parents giving into and exploit the requirements of a so-called "golden child" by taking on the role of the "scapegoat child" and "invisible child." Those services were not intended to help children in any way. However, there are also positions that children in narcissistic families must fill to appease the parent. Since they themselves were the ones most affected by their dysfunctional culture, children of crazy families in their own right took on tasks of their own to relieve their suffering.

The four additional roles of children in narcissistic communities are: "hero/responsible child," "caretaker/ placate," "mascot/clown," and "mastermind/manipulator." Children can assume one or more of these roles. "Only children" appear to carry on several tasks in order to respond to their feelings.

The Caretaker/Parenting Service Acceptor Boy

The caretaker/placate child assumes the position of the family emotional guardian. He struggles with the ever-changing moods and emotions of his kin. His strengths are listening, helping, nurturing, and therapy in every case.

This child has a delicate, peaceful, and pacifying state of nature. His calming spirit cannot withstand an intense argument or chaotic circumstance. When family problems emerge, or when he feels that they are about to, his personality automatically switches to pacifying mode.

The caretaker used this line on a sensitive client but claimed he does not accept or require any emotional assistance from the client himself. He has not found successful strategies to satisfy his own desires, but he appears to concentrate more of his energy on satisfying his family members' needs.

This boy was a "pleaser." He still wanted to do with someone something they could not or wouldn't do themselves. He is a selfless person who may offer affection but does not know how to reciprocate it. The caring, supportive and encouraging attention aimed at him will lead him to feel insecure and feel like he is the one seeking support. When he is relaxed, he is the one to send and not the recipient.

Throughout a child's lifespan, the caretaker is believed to have been a savior. Friendships and collaborations become construction ventures. Whatever the essence of the friendship, his task is to repair people, to stop them from moving down a poor road. These partnerships are also poisonous, abusive and seem to make their life miserable.

In adulthood, the caretaker is likely to pursue a job in a manner that is similar to what he needs to do, depending on the knowledge that he has gained in his past life. However, he will never be willing to use his own caring natures but will instead find it impossible to recognize and fulfill his own desires. He is sure to be exploited, no matter his acts, and he is quick to exploit.

The Weird Googly-Eyed Guy

The mascot or clown is closer to but not necessarily the youngest kid in the household. In children with a mental disorder, social well-being is treated very seriously, in a manner that suits a child's nature versus the way a caretaker handles a child. Families who have a toddler with ADHD typically require a social operator_directing them in everyday life to divert the family's focus away from the frustration and rage that occurs. He is their family member who is most reliable at raising their moods and helping them feel stronger.

It seems that his disposition is what one would term "Happy-Go-Lucky," of which a fast demeanor is most definitely part of his "React-Before-Think" existence. The mascot plays a comical role in her traumatic reality, helps to deflect it, and communicates his agony with his laughter. When he and his friends don't get their way at home and at school, parents can quickly convey her frustration and disappointment, as well as sadness and powerlessness.

He makes people laugh at him as an object of mockery by self-deprecating humor, often ditsy actions, or foolishness. He adopts an identity in public events that is that of a blackly-comedic human being, with no one taking him seriously.

As adults, they live rewarding lives and take pleasure in amplifying the pain of others through laughter. While one has pleasure and satisfaction, they may lose out on this. Using certain individuals, suppression of their own suffering from the "safe" zone of their brains contributes to persistent depression. They would never be able to establish an authentic self when they don't really have an authentic identity, to begin with.

The quick-witted, deceptive boy

Unlike the three other roles, the mastermind/manipulator garners no positive qualities from society. He is really irresponsible, deceitful, and rude.

The mastermind determines what the family thinks. He is cunning, much like the stinging insect. He takes his issues on to somebody else to fix by exploiting them.

The culprit's manipulations are motivated by haughty feelings of becoming a rightful individual, much like the narcissist himself. He is an opportunistic individual, letting out an overwhelming amount of shamelessness when it comes to serving his own desires, but can still be regarded as shrewd enough.

He exploits the instability of his family so that he can take advantage of it. This child's family members are really vulnerable, but he capitalizes on their vulnerabilities to get what he needs. He will haunt the family unit, causing conflict and sometimes triangulating insincere charm; but he never succeeds. When it comes to his diplomatic skills, he has an inherent, mastered capacity to trick people into doing his bidding. The relatives do occasionally pick on to what his ploys are but are unwilling to cope with his deceptive skills.

It is accurate that the mastermind can even wear a mascot outfit much like the mascot, but his humor is more cynical and caustic than calming. Any of the senator's committee comments appear to come off as attention-seeking, deficient in emotional security, and a cover-up for his own insecurities. It is normal for masterminds to strike by asking. He is planning for the portion of his life that he will have to perform in adulthood–with possibly the same outcomes.

Regardless of how often one is prepared to cope with them, adolescents in sexually abusive/narcissistic homes can become lifetime mental templates for others, which can contribute to continued violence and domination. Relationships, families, parenting, scholastic endeavor, and professions would also be in danger from a genetically engineered unhealthy method of communicating.

Children who grow up in narcissistic households also endure tremendous violence from their parents. Good lifestyle coping habits that are inborn can never be taught. As a consequence of their environment, certain children cannot help but cope in ways, including by choosing to use comedy to help them cope. Currently, the coping strategies employed for children affected by ADHD are seldom maladaptive; it is these dysfunctional and unhealthy methods that these children would continue to employ as adults.

1.15 Why Do Narcissistic Parents Behave Like This?

During childhood, a child lacks the ability to understand his narcissistic parents' actions. They spend their childhood with no affection, care, generosity and are exploited emotionally, physically, and mentally. The coping mechanisms are employed, which makes people stay away from any emotional pain.

Narcissistic parents are rarely available with no feelings, and this makes a child crave love, intimacy, and respect. It is difficult to talk with the parent as they are abusive. The only way to control these feelings is to ignore them. This reduces pain. Since they were behaving badly from an early age, they changed into lying, manipulative and disrespectful persons. Their dreams will not be fulfilled.

Narcissists often suffer from traumatic experiences as children, and this causes them to be depressed and self-pity. They can deal with this situation in a constructive manner by turning off their sympathies. Whenever they had strong feelings, they were told to suppress them. These people fear that they are at risk of exploitation.

1.16 How Do Abusive Parents Abuse Their Kids and Punish Them?

Narcissistic abuse is different from physical abuse. The wounds are deeper yet invisible. There are no bruises, broken bones, or bandages. The verbal and emotional abuse that toxic parents inflict upon a child happens slowly but has long-lasting effects. It's an insidious, progressive breakdown of self-worth and identity. This makes the victim think that something went wrong with genes.

Abusive parent has many forms of abusing and punishing his or her kid. Here are some common ways in which narcissists use them.

1. ***Emotional Slander:*** The narcissistic mother or father would use every imaginable way to get what she or he wants. Narcissists blackmail others by manipulating their emotions. There are several reasons in which they manipulate their children as their property.
2. ***Excessive parental control:*** By manipulating every step a child takes and behaviors. A child will have no confidence as they cannot live alone. He is all dependent on his parents at the cost of his self-worth and self-esteem. He also develops insecurities.
3. ***Claiming success:*** So, if a child achieves something, then such parents claim the credit for his all achievements. A child is indebted to be thankful and should perform better for his parents. This makes a child stressed and race-fatigue.
4. ***No recognition of emotions:*** narcissistic parent ignores child's feelings, dreams, and passion. They will never acknowledge a child's likes.

1.17 Which Issues Adult Child Have?

Children of narcissistic parents develop psychological, emotional, and physical disorders. As they nurture with no affections, care, and emotional attachment. A few issues are as follows

- Childhood trauma or complex PTSD.

- Negative vibes.

- Inter-dependency.

- Intense guilty.

- Ignore their own existence for other's validation.

- Trust issues.

- Stress issues.

- Unhealthy relationships.

- Becomes narcissistic if the golden child.

- Accepts that his parent doesn't love like other parents.

1.18 How to Deal Narcissistic Parent

Dealing with narcissist parents, it is almost assured that they still have any presence in a child's existence, even if it's just the simplest and subtle. Most narcissistic individuals are advised not to have much interaction with those parents. In this way, a child can begin his healing by doing the following:

- Avoid waiting for a parent to change — it will never happen.

- Enable to weep for the birth of parents they had never raised to hide natural emotions. Today is a pleasant time to welcome those suppressed emotions and memories.

- Adopt self-care.

- Develop self-love

- Listen to the inner child to mature

- Keep a regular diary of accomplishments. This will make me more conscious.

- Work on inner development shows the frustration that a child has inside correctly and properly.

- Doing anything to benefit people close to a child is a really healthy thing to do.

- Utilize books.

Chapter 2: Proof That Monsters Do Exist-If Mother Is Narcissistic

2.1 Mother A True Soulmate

Mother is our first-ever and a very important source of love. She is the heart and soul of life. She is a link between us and the world. Every individual desires physical and emotional protection and nourishment. Mother is considered a torchbearer in darkness, the center of life, flower in spring, and a sweater in winters, and water in summers in one's life. One cannot simply deny the importance of a mother in the early upbringing of a child. They might be considered ordinary in everyday life but are as magical as the ocean to every child. Healthy mothers reorient themselves while raising children. Like a soul mate, the mother transforms the existence of a child over and over again endlessly and effortlessly. She undertakes to enhance a child's knowledge, wisdom, skills, and physical development; a continuous and lifelong process. This makes the mother and child connection deep, remarkable, and unique.

2.2 Mother-Child Bonding

Mothers and their newborns are strongly likely to be bonded immediately after birth. As soon as the two are brought together, trust begins to build. Besides breastfeeding, the mother frequently holds the infant near her for the first precious hours and days of her life.

Even in the case where mothers and babies are separated after birth due to health or logistical reasons, they can still bond. In this case, close contact between mothers and infants leads to negative effects.

There should be no pressure from mothers for sudden bonding with babies in the first few months. Instead of doing harm to her child, she sets up a long-term bond with him by giving her child excuses to trust her.

2.3 Mother-Child Attachment

When toddlers become preschoolers, they know their mothers are their primary individuals to meet their needs, and the initial bonding cycle has been completed. At this point, toddlers realize that they are individuals and are able to set their own limits.

As a child explores to test his/her mother's boundaries, a child will eventually learn to trust his mother again. In this way, the newborns will attach more strongly to their mothers after the first stage of bonding is completed.

While a discussion of a child's relationship with their mother can certainly be extremely psychological or sociological, it does not have to be. In my opinion, none of the mothers and children can discuss anything seriously.

It is natural for new mothers to fear "messing up" or somehow "ruining" their children, but in most cases reconnecting after childbirth is a natural process. Mothers need not worry about whether they have a good relationship with their children or not—there is no external standard by which they must perform. Instead, mothers should follow their instinctual feelings, and as long as they are happy, the quality of their children is likely to be high too.

The bond of mother and child is even before birth. Those months mark the most challenging but worthy relationship. In the mental, emotional, social, and physical development of a child, one cannot deny mothers' significance. This develops a strong emotional bond between mother and child.

Whoever gives the motherly attachment to the child (caretaker, nuns, grandparents), the emotional bond is developed, which is observed even when a child gets mature.

Forming an attachment with their children involves:

- Hug them.

- Healthy environment.

- Talk to them.

- Play with them.

- Laugh with them.

- Sleep on time.

- Eating habits should be monitored.

- Set limits to educate manners.

- Learning their feelings (i.e., facial expressions, sounds they make, how they communicate their needs).

2.4 Eight Different Roles of a Mother in Child Development

Child development includes physical, social, emotional, and cognitive/mental aspects. Children need all the support they can get, and the one person who has the most influence on children is the mother. It is the mother's responsibility to be the primary caregiver in both traditional and single-parent families. Mothers are in the unique position of influencing children's development in all areas, starting with the time of bonding and attachments.

There is a great deal they do for their child, unknowingly and knowingly. As a mother, they will fulfill eight kinds of roles in their child's growth and development.

Emotional Attachment

As a mother and the primary caregiver in her child's earliest days, weeks and months, she is her first link of attachment. Her baby will learn his emotions related to his mother through interaction between them.

How she bonds with her child during the infant stage will deeply impact their development as an adult. The mother-child relationship one creates during the earliest years is closely linked to how the child is socially and emotionally well-adjusted later on in life. As a mother, it is important how quickly she reacts to her child's needs and the way to satisfy those needs.

Trust and security

She needs to understand the importance of mothers in child development. The other skill is trust, as her child will learn this from her.

As a mother, she has to teach her child the virtue of integrity. If her child can trust her, then he will become emotionally secure.

Children need the support and encouragement of their parents in order to succeed. Mother's encouragement will show the child that her love for him is constant, and it will show him that he is safe with her forever.

Sentimental

There will be times where nothing will seem to be going according to plan. It's a natural reaction to anger and frustration to give up hope. Think of her child's perspective. Her child will learn a big lesson in life by listening to her thoughts and showing kindness.

As a mother, she may have a different perspective and way of tackling things, while her child may have an entirely different idea and perception. She needs to understand a child's perspective too. She better teaches him the consequences of doing something wrong or making the wrong decisions.

Kind and affectionate

The way she treats her child will shape the child's development throughout his childhood and his adult years.

Always treat children with kindness, regardless of how much stress and anger is going on in life. Her response to the child's needs on a daily basis and activities will show him the importance of love towards others.

The manner in which she talks to her child will positively affect the child's attitude towards others.

Being Together

She teaches the importance of family to her child through her social interaction and association with other family members.

Introduce kids to different family members and take them to different outings. Have family time at home regularly.

Optimism

Life may be hard, but how she deals with hardship can show the child how important a positive attitude is. Her child can see that having a positive attitude helps to overcome difficulties.

Always teach a child to be optimistic. It is beneficial for a child to learn from his wrong-doing and to never lose hope.

Hard Work

It takes the most experience to teach hard work. Her performance for the child's development is the biggest example for him in front of him.

A child may think it is hard work to go to school. Remind a child that it is a positive thing for him to take care of him/herself.

Discipline

- Their child will always be at ease if he follows set routines.
- Teach their child how to manage time effectively by following a routine.
- Make sure their kids learn the importance of discipline and have routines in their daily lives.

2.5 If the Mother Is Suffering from the Narcissistic Syndrome

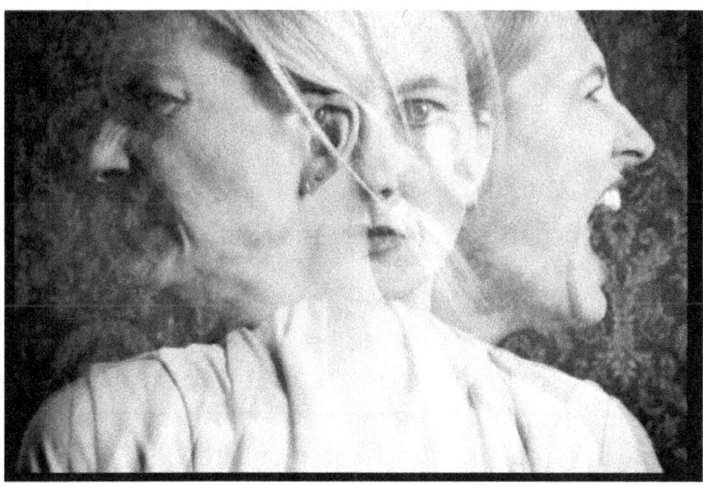

Healthy mothers come home and support their kids, but don does not control them. At the same time, narcissistic mothers continue to need attention and control, even at home. If the mother is narcissistic, the key element is that she has little patience or empathy for her children's independent and demanding needs.

It is important to know what NPD is. Narcissistic personality disorder (NPD) is a personality disorder with traits of demanding attention, lacking empathy and emotions for others. Research has also found a less-extreme form of narcissism that is termed narcissistic personality type. Individuals who possess characteristics of narcissistic personality disorder are considered normal beings.

People use this term to describe those who are narcissistic, lack empathy, and are constantly seeking praise. These behaviors are not pleasant. Treating this disorder can be difficult. Criteria include loss of feelings for others and limited ability to understand what others are experiencing. Most NPD moms do not meet clinical criteria for NPD.

Narcissistic mothers are not aware of their own feelings. They will never consider another's feelings. They have no clue how a kid's life is like. Kids may be affected in many ways. Despite being sensitive to judgment and criticism, they tend to criticize and judge others.

The world will embrace her, but still, she behaves as self-centered and easily annoyed. She may be loved by her friends and colleagues, but they don't know the mother a child knows. A child gets maternal love occasionally but is punctuated by control, anger and needs to be dependent. This very nature of a mother drags a child to think of being helpless. A child is living in a cage which is provided with every facility for physical nourishment but with strong and long iron rods not to think or make decisions of their own.

Children do not immediately recognize that their mother's confidence is fragile. Because she needs to be right, he is trained to please his egoistic mother.

2.6 If a Child has a narcissistic mother, He didn´t Get a mother

A narcissistic mother is not truly a mother. She does not really parent her children and has no room for compassion, love, and care for them in the true sense. She only showers her love when she wants something to be done of her choice. It's always about her and about children.

She projects herself onto children. A minor mistake gives her the right to attack and embarrass them with her rage. She will take credit for any achievement of her children or blame them for any failure. She even sets sibling rivalry due to jealousy or insecurity. This shatters the confidence, personality, and dignity of children.

2.7 How Children Are Affected

Children raised in homes dominated by narcissistic mothers may go through a roller coaster of emotions during their childhood. Due to feeling guilty for past deeds, they spend their time trying to please their mothers.

Rather than loving and accepting their child for who they are, their judgmental mother only criticizes them to the point that their self-esteem becomes completely shattered. They will be treated as if they have a terrible character. They will be told that they are not enough; they will feel that no one else will do for them what they want to be done, and for narcissistic mothers, they will never be enough.

They will spend the rest of their lives lacking approval and desperately trying to get approval. Some will turn to therapy for help, some will become narcissists themselves, some will subconsciously seek out narcissistic partners in their children's lives, and some will become narcissistic parents.

2.8 Adults Often Become Too Caring

Pathological caretaking involves a kid (and eventually an adult) becoming devoted to a parent's needs and attuning to the parent's feelings while simultaneously suppressing their own.

These children grew up in a narcissistic environment, which caused them to be distressed and live-in poverty. Another problem that occurred to these children is a Depleted Subjective World.

As adults, narcissist children frequently find themselves in relationships where they are subjected to "fulfilling mental states for others while also experiencing a sense of shame correlated with their own emotions and desires."

The consequence is a "Wounded Identity" because of the neglect and wounds that the abusive parent has left on the developing infant.

As adults, narcissistic children commonly encounter them in relationships in which they are subjected to "fulfilling mental states for others while also having a sense of shame correlated with their own thoughts and wants." They are ambitious but will often burn themselves out because they are not committed to their career path. Their parents' narcissism often influences their ambitions in life.

In a fight for self-definition and genuine control, children whose mothers have become narcissistic are trapped. To rediscover oneself takes several years.

2.9. Adult Faces the Shame

People who narcissistic parents abused experience chronic shame, but children of narcissists tend to have the most severe case of chronic shame known to the field of psychology.

Narcissistic parents translate their own guilt on their children as an extension of their shame-foaming and may even utilize shame as a protective tactic. They are leaving their kids with the extreme and toxic emotional fallout of guilt by using shame as a way to monitor their children.

Narcissistic parents usually do not try to repair the parent-child attachment. They neglect their children's emotional needs, and in so doing, they leave them to take on the burden of stress relating to their emotions alone, when they would normally have an adult to help. Sometimes children who already have mental illnesses may experience hallucinations and dissociative states to explain away actual symptoms they are experiencing.

Shame impacts our sense of self and relationships and can impair our ability to form healthy relationships. Due to the parents' narcissistic tendencies, children of narcissists often perceive themselves to be defective.

Within the sense of identity, these people often feel empty spaces.

Their sense of self is disrupted, often because of psychosis, but forgotten painful experiences can also "hijack" victims and transfer them to previous traumatic experiences from the present moment and back.

2.10 Children of Narcissistic Mothers

Abusers project their feelings of failure and rejection onto their children, often resulting in narcissism and chronic shame. The child will experience shame when they fail to live up to the "idealized" parent.

The narcissistic parent will "feel threatened" and envious of a child's ability to be dependent on them. The narcissistic parent, dependent on a child, will oppose any form of independence or standing in their own sovereignty.

When children have narcissistic parents, they must "forget" or hide their genuine needs and wants in order to "serve" their parents in a self-sacrificing (self-widowed) nature; they are no longer able to be self-sufficient individuals.

2.11 Disorders Due to Narcissistic Mothers

Children are very close to their mother if they do not receive true affection, care, and positive vibes from them, then develop invisible wounds. But mothers having a hidden scar satisfy their egos through their children. As a result, children suffer from mental disorders.

1. OCD
2. C-PTSD

OCD

A child may develop something called Symmetry and Order OCD (excessive thinking (obsessions) that contribute to repeated habits (compulsions)).

The fear of Symmetry OCD suffers will become fixated with the location of certain objects, such as pillows, and will feel anxious and disturbed when seeing certain objects that are not aligned properly or seem somehow incomplete.

Those who strive to pursue exactness about all aspects, whether it is money, art, or order, may experience intense anxiety, an extreme response, and an urgent desire or need to find "balance" regarding the "symmetry" within a circumstance.

Treatment

Infants are managed using occupational counseling and prescribed drugs. Behavior counseling, like cognitive behavioral therapy (CBT), makes the infant turn harmful ideas into more productive, more optimistic modes of thinking and these thoughts contribute to more effective behavior. Behavior treatment for adolescents involves introducing them to their fears when they mature into young adulthood in a healthy atmosphere to make them realize that negative outcomes don't normally emerge as a consequence of their behavior because they don't really do what they believe they are doing. Behavior counseling itself is successful, but certain children need medication to be administered to be efficient for both behavior therapy and medicine. Both family and schools may help children relieve tension by being a part of the counseling method and understanding how to act supportively without being unwittingly causing further strain for the kid to move into another compulsion mode.

C-PTSD

Past scholars have usually paid greater attention to the consequences of traumatic incidents like collisions, conflicts, and natural disasters. Iraq was really harsh on our troops physically, but not so hard on their emotional well-being, yet now that they are safe, it seems that Post Traumatic Stress Disorder is a more fitting term (PTSD). "Complex PTSD" is a word employed for defining a child's childhood trauma that happens in an unconscious way, such as maternal deprivation. It is also named invisible trauma.

When it comes to child neglect, there are several ways of detection. But, in these situations, the issues that derive from an incompetent or defective adult also only appear to the community. Trauma often happens because one or more health professionals fall shy to meet the needs of a loved one for care and treatment.

In a family environment or situation that is tense or prone to tension, certain children may tend to feel trapped into a depression or an emotional withdrawal where they have to "take on more adult" responsibilities or feel a sense of becoming black-sheep, the unpopular boy. This is a vulnerable and intense family dynamics that can be very detrimental to a child. They may be in an oppressive loop or even a self-perpetuating cycle of trying to be better but only being able to measure up to the standards set for them.

As parents, these are some of the benefits coming from raising a young, sensitive and talented child. However, they must demonstrate a very mature and high degree of understanding. A lot of parents struggle to be the way they should be. Much of the time, parents should not neglect or assault their children because they are not that trained or experienced and they are more often affected by unexpected emotional circumstances.

In serious situations, the individuals who come into contact with emotionally intense children end up (so to speak) in one of two states; they either impale their own love for a child or hate a child for its strangeness.

PTSD signs in infants and adolescents

- Ignoring circumstances that may cause their trauma.

- Hallucinations may occur.

- Playing through the pain over and over again.

- Reckless.

- Worried sometimes.

- Emotionless.

- Losing concentration at college.

Children who have PTSD signs would usually vanish after a few months. It should not mean that a child needs not to see a doctor for an evaluation and explore medical plans should problems arise. PTSD is treatable, but if the child needs assistance, ask for it. A brief list of popular PTSD care services for children.

Cognitive-behavioral treatment is a method of talk therapy, and this trauma-focused type may be done on adults and adolescents. A CBT therapist helps a child recognize and alter unfounded or illogical feelings regarding the abuse itself or about individuals and circumstances. In addition to the above-listed material, several patients obtain CBT.

Play counseling will perform best with younger children who fail to express their responses to the trauma and awareness of what occurred. Play therapists utilize painting, toys, and other strategies to help children process traumas and deal with life.

Eye gestures desensitization and reprocessing (EMDR) is a method increasingly utilized by mental health practitioners. Therapies include directed eye control techniques as an infant recalls the stressful experience and works with feelings around it.

There is no drug that "cures" PTSD, although several drugs can alleviate the problems of some children when they are still seeing a doctor.

PTSD effects can often be induced by other conditions and may often result in opioid usage, unhealthy habits, and self-injury. Issues would continue to be resolved in therapy to support their child to achieve a complete recovery.

2.12 Children Raised by Narcissistic Mothers Hardly Get Over the Rage

Getting over frustration needs comprehension. Children try to recognize the facts regarding their mother. Since the child has gone through trauma for a long time, that is why he feels gloomy and desires loneliness. Forgiveness is the secret of releasing bad emotions. When the child forgives, he will allow himself free from the process of being tainted with lust for her. If he does not accept, rage and animosity may dwell inside, triggering frustration and hostility

Chapter 3: Toxic Mothers Exposed

3.1 Characteristics of Narcissistic Mothers

A narcissistic mother craves attention, whether it comes from charm, beauty, intelligence, or financial prowess. She might be a charming, a chutzpah woman and an authoritative position to be admired, but the family is a spectator of the coin's coarse side. Kids of toxic mothers live an upset and astray life and search for love from others, which they never receive from home. Children expect a normal upbringing as healthy parents provide, but they are not given the affection and back when facing a narcissistic mother.

Narcissistic mothers will often have extreme self-concern and self-image. She cannot even provide her children with the basic social help they need to develop up to be well-adjusted adults.

Narcissists may become "narcissistic" over the slightest thing, which results in their children being belittled, abused emotionally, and sometimes physically abused. The standard manipulative mother, regardless of conditions, is almost difficult to satisfy. She also snuffs or disregards her children's love attempts.

For the same purposes, a good individual has no children in a selfish mother. She doesn't expect to see their births look and see their personality grow.

She has them solely to gaze at herself in order to get more mirrors, in order to want tiny miniatures from herself. She resents all the jobs she worries about and views it as a responsibility. She "hands-offs" child-rearing to a child itself, improperly, as quickly as it can.

A narcissistic mother could show across as a nurturing, compassionate mum, but she has an exclusive and possessively tight relationship with her children to exploit and dominate them. While most parents watch a child's freedom with joy, a narcissistic parent feels an utter act of treason, any move away.

The manifestations of a manipulative mother include the usual lies and the infant's relentless criticism as a loving mom. She makes it plain orally and nonverbally, in no uncertain words, that they are not as successful as others.

Her narcissistic tenders may not cease in infancy but begin to intervene and hurt her self-esteem and whatever friendship they might have.

Children with abusive parents also have trouble establishing stable partnerships and are more prone to develop depression and anxiety.

Following are the signs that a child is dealing with a narcissistic mother.

3.1.1. Can do Anything

There is often a reason or justification. Cruelty is disguised with passion. Aggressive action is presented as thoughtful. Deceptions are viewed as gifts. It is masked as caring. She does what's best for them. She needs to support everyone.

She never suggests that she feels he is deficient. After kids give her a compliment, she will always react by criticizing the sibling, avoiding kids, or belittling kids for a short period to know that it is not okay to be proud of themselves. She reacts and targets at the right time so that others become aware of her fall/ defame.

She also makes fun of women, suggesting that they're lesser. She can speak about what a great job somebody else did or how highly she thinks about them. They should pick one of them. She told kids that they are not nice without getting up a phrase. This can ruin the fun and pleasure in a partnership, as described earlier. Narcissists may take advantage of instilling an awful and vocal response in a child without a phrase. As a consequence, kids are always in the wrong, always terrified, and can never find out why.

This lady's abusiveness is part of a lifetime of systematic control and exploitation, and it is almost hard to describe to most people what is so horrible about her. Around the same time, she behaves carefully when engaged in aggressive conduct. Abusers are also secretive, so-to-speak. The precise dates and occasions for her wrongdoing are deliberately planned in such a manner that she may not be identified. Study findings indicate that children of abusive parents regularly complain that no one trusts them! Sadly, psychiatrists will often side with narcissists when they blame the survivor.

3.1.2. Ignore rights

Kids sound like a part of her. Their property has been moved without notice or permission. When anyone hits their meal, it becomes theirs. Their land will be repossessed even without any notice. She dominates kids only because she has been granted power. Kids are talked to as if they do not exist. Kids are not getting alone time in the shower or apartment because she continuously barges her into their world. She has got nosy traits and asks all the way. She would still seek out derogatory knowledge regarding kids, which she will leverage against them. She does stuff against kid's will on a daily basis. This is seen without any indication of shame or hesitation.

Every effort to stay independent on the kid's part would be firmly resisted. If kids choose to be independent, they can wear age-appropriate clothes; it is their preference.

3.1.3. Biasness

Narcissistic mothers are generally blamed for selecting one (sometimes more) infant to be the golden child and another one (sometimes more) to be the scapegoat. Narcissism is helping others in exchange for getting advantages. Many of the families would have to raise the Little Prince. The scapegoat gets the favor and profit without needing to fight for it. The golden boy has no flaws. The scapegoat still carries the weight of obligation. This decreases sibling ties and leads children to confrontation. The group would be strongly dominated by the narcissist and his unfairness. The gold child will profit from this scenario by accusing the scapegoat of the mother's attitude. He will physically harm the scapegoat as well, so the selfish mother doesn't have to.

3.1.4. Undermine others

Kid's contributions are remembered to a large degree by just the extent that she will claim credit for them. Something that she is unwilling to do is dismissed or deflated. Whatever the situation, this sweetie can keep annoying kids at all conceivable stages. She threatens the kid by irritating or provoking disputes with him until he is in a position where he needs to achieve something. She still gets irritated and annoyed if he prefers anything/ anyone to her. She can be mean about stuff that is far from performance in an effort to tarnish the satisfaction of what she has achieved. Regardless of his achievements, she will still remind him of their shortcomings.

3.1.5. Critique

She lets him feel why she dislikes him in several respects. If he inquires of mistreatment by someone else, she will advocate on behalf of that person even if she is not connected to them at all. She is not dealing with disappointed citizens or their grievances injustice. She also needs to let him realize that he is still mistaken.

She can offer generalized barbs that are almost impossible to rebut (always in a loving, compassionate tone). She will administer slams in a sidelong manner. This helps the reader to convey critique while staying ambiguous.

She can eventually join the discussion by sharing little information about something she did that he or she liked. She will hint to him that her relationship with another guy is great because his relationship with her isn't – the unspoken implication being that he does not mean anything to her.

She refuses, denies, denies. Her disrespect for what he suggests that he just garbage. She didn't listen to a bit of what he said.

3.1.6. Imbalances life

An offender might say stuff like "he makes things up" to invalidate his experience of violence. She can appear not to recall perhaps the most famous incidents, flatly refusing that they actually existed or that she may have forgotten. This is an offensive technique called "gas lighting," and this is particularly popular among offenders of all forms. He gets confused because his assumptions have been undermined. He gets the feeling that he is not as successful at logic as he once was. It renders him more open to the violent guy.

Narcissists do this frequently. The narcissist can make think that he is unstable if he disagrees with his/her suggestions. He is insecure. He is wrong. He is extremely emotional. He is just unfair. When he is calmer, she can speak to him. She might also suspect him of being neurotic or psychotic.

She would distribute negative remarks towards others to be deliberately hurtful and to receive support from some. She did nothing. So, she doesn't realize that he is upset with her. He also harmed her gravely. She suggests that he may like a psychotherapist. She likes him so much but doesn't know what to do. I just don't need his support. He knows.

She has related his animosity to his intrinsic moral defects and compromised his reputation with her listeners. She represents the caring mother so beautifully that no one will ever think otherwise.

3.1.7. Envious

When anything good happens to others, her jealousy will make itself known. She could rob his valuables or cheat him. She is still dreaming about opportunities to have what others have. Narcissistic mothers also jockey for influence with their children or daughters-in-law. They'll bar their daughters from wearing lipstick, following conventional Islamic ways, or to date. They would condemn their daughter's and daughters-in-looks. Law's Jealousy is popular in partnerships and has several forms. Narcissistic mothers reportedly threaten to disrupt their children's interactions and meddle with the schooling of their grandchildren.

3.1.8. Cheats

Whenever she speaks to something of deep emotional attachment, she's definitely misleading. Overstepping the boundaries of deception is one of the main characteristics that distinguish a narcissist. She would lie about her relationship with them, about her relationship with him, or about some circumstance with him so as to make herself seem even stronger than she actually is.

Narcissists are often very particular when they tell lies. She'll utter a convincing fib in an attempt to make up whether she's faced with her lie. She provides an updated edition of his letter that he would approve of. She alleges that he did stuff that he didn't. She will lie to lessen the information until she really has it. This is because the most gullible of her peers would never even consider that this is immoral.

She would quickly lie to him. She says that she is unable to recall what she did wrong or what she has achieved in the past. Suppose he cannot use figures of speech. His discussions with her are casually brusque and don't owe her ample consideration to achieve a proper impression. He is now participating in a game where there is just one rule: he can't win.

She would bluntly refute that she said something false. She fears that she may have done something wrong. The misconduct is most definitely whitewashed to make things look stronger. Her contradictions include saying "I guess" and "maybe" because she really understands what she is talking about.

3.1.9. Wants to be in the spotlight

The goal of narcissistic mothers is for their children to be recognizable and be at the center of focus. Narcissistic mothers love their children and often pepper them with petty demands. As he couldn't be told what to do at the start of the day, but he was obligated to perform it at the discretion of his mum.

Narcissistic mothers have the propensity to render the center of their festivities. She might like entertaining because she can be the life of every crowd. She will try to steal the limelight from everyone she can, especially her child. She also goes anywhere where she is not welcome. If he sees her, he will visit her daily. Entertaining herself is nonsensical. Throughout my youth and adolescence, she was my first encouragement, giving me true love, devotion, and support.

As the depressive mothers grow older, they resort to dramatizing all and finally wind up getting themselves sick. This offers them the ability to create a high income when they are liable for his growth as an infant. Whenever this occurs, they will then contact him to demand him to testify at the hearing as soon as practicable. Because of his age, it is difficult for him to treat them since he cannot simply deny it. If he is not offering to the crowd, he is seeking to win over, and it's possibly time to leave. The habits prevalent in narcissistic women with Alzheimer's may be often displayed.

3.1.10. Controls

She can take advantage of his emotions. Parents are so mentally manipulative that their kids sometimes term them mental vampires. She does stuff that is wounding or irritating or suspicious to him, and all the while has a grin in her smile. His mother might have brought him to horror movies and told terrifying things. Then, she could have ridiculed him as he called out for her affection. He can detect the scorn in her accent as she teases him or does disturbing stuff to him. After she'll chat about how bad she hurt him, enthusiastically showing him how much fun, she is to mess around and inviting others to participate in her fun. She loves her brutality and little feeling of remorse. She needs him to realize that his misery makes her proud. She may be a tough person to stop. This is simple mental violence. She feeds off of the suffering.

This may be known as emotional vampirism as there is a sort of sadism mixed with it. When selfish mothers get upset, they also stage self-pitying dramas. Through her deep sorrow, she cries that she cannot survive anymore. She needs to finish her marriage. The consequence of her self-pity would be felt deeply by her peers and other people. Narcissists often engage themselves in traumatic or stressful incidents.

3.1.11. Stubborn

She still does something unique. She likes still to get her own way. She does whatever she wishes without worrying about the consequences. She would try her absolute best to get him what he desires, particularly though it was completely his privilege to do so and even though she was unfair. If he informs her that she can't bring her friends to his house, she will turn up regardless, and she will think up a story about why the party has been postponed.

Narcissists are really poor at creating presents. The sooner he offers as a present to someone, the more they will give to him as a gift later. She can say no when she needs to say yes. She could provide a gift or get him a gift in order to make herself feel better, and get a gift for herself at the same time.

3.1.12. Selfish

She is really significant, taking priority over his needs. Her survival is evidently at risk, and she cannot be overlooked any longer. She still gets her way, even though she is making unfair requests. She will judge incessantly, considering how poor her own condition is. If he finds out the problem with her, she can spontaneously, thoughtlessly sweep it away as of no significance.

3.1.13. Easily Annoyed

If kids displease or defy her, she will become angry with indignation, attack, rage, wind, confine, place her child outside in poor weather or engage in violence.

3.1.14. Scared

For crime victims, threats and manipulation are successful ways of manipulating their attacker. The narcissist teaches to dread their rage

Even though they're not physically there. Another choice is quiet. If someone gives a woman everything, she desires all the time, the woman will finally stop moaning because she feels satisfied. If not, retribution will be administered. The adult children of narcissists are still really afraid of her. A narcissistic mother will turn it on with a pause or a look that shows kids her displeasure with her.

Narcissists can find several different methods to coerce and overpower others. They look for a way to get their anger out at kids. They definitely would not have been beaten, but they were neglected in a case where a typical mother would have shown any sort of concern. She utilizes this non-violent method of battery to help hide the aggressive conduct from her partner. They consume so much and are fat. She resents having to take care of kids. They have a lot of nerve to get sick and add burdens to her.

Narcissistic mothers often abuse if they lose someone on them or if a regular mother doesn't protect them. Even the golden kid of the narcissist is allowed to exploit the scapegoat. Narcissists also utilize abuse to expose kids. She made sure they are noticed one of their siblings getting beaten. She quickly placed Mom's fear into them without lifting a fist.

3.1.15. Childlike behavior

Narcissistic mothers are typically only infantile. If he fails to let her force her to do anything, she will cry because kids don't value her, and they will do what she wishes if they valued her. If they damage her emotions, she will shock them violently that they are sorry that they did not treat her well while she is gone. This kid's grievances and replies may sound absurd, but the narcissist is gone. As a girl, if he asks her to avoid any inappropriate behavior, she will explain it by pointing out what she believes he has done is identical, as though a child's childhood behavior is cause for an adult's childhood conduct. "Getting even" is more of her interactions with kids. Whenever they refuse to give her the love, attention, or service that she thinks she needs, or her desires are frustrated, she must demonstrate it to them.

3.1.16. Furious

She doesn't inquire. She doesn't ask. She wonders. She makes outrageous demands, and if she knows she will get away with it, she can take whatever she likes. Her children's expectations and her critiques are posed in a rather offensive fashion. She will not make a comment, press and twist and trick to send them in.

3.1.17. Prettification

She is willing; she shoves her obligations to them so that they can take care of themselves as best they can. She declined medical attention, sufficient clothes, transportation, or simple comforts, something she would never have contemplated giving up. She never gave a birthday party or allowed them to sleep. In her home, their buddies were never invited. She did not want to take them somewhere, but they turned down invites since they have no means to get here.

Even if she could comfortably afford it, she might not purchase their school photos. They have a niggardly wardrobe supplement or purchased them the cheapest clothes she might have without being humiliated. Any order for equipment, clothes or toiletries from school was satisfied as soon as got a job. They educated themselves at colleges and chose a discount without visiting them. They signed up for the SATs, received the money to pay, and spoke to someone to drive them to the test spot. They worked three jobs in this cheap school, and eventually, she chirped at him when he had mononucleosis that she was "so happy he could be caring." She even offered them duties that were her own right and could not have been forced on a child.

3.1.18. Manipulative

She is exploitative. She is trying to cheat to get jobs, income, or stuff she needs for nothing from other people. Of course, this involves her son. If she opened a bank account for him, she was a trustee with the power to remove money from the account. She pulled it out when he poured money into it. Maybe his identification has been compromised. She took him to draw upon her income taxes, so even without submitting her to criminal sanctions, he couldn't file separately. When she had an understanding with him, the minute she didn't fulfill her interests was broken. When he is lifted it to insist that it stick to that deal, she shrugged off and disciplined him afterward so he couldn't defy it again.

The narcissist often harnesses an infant in order to absorb punishment from an oppressive parent. The husband comes home in a drunken fury, and the mother instantly complains about the boy's wrongdoing. The selfish mother often merely uses the infant to sustain a sick marriage because the alternative is divorced or because he needs to go to work. The child is annoyed, but the mother never knows, or worse, when she informs the mother about the irritation, she considers a child a liar.

3.1.19. Prefer Looks

It sounds a little of a psycho-babble, but narcissists do it all. Research suggests she is trying to place her own negative behavior, character, and characteristics on them to deny them in herself and blame them. It can be really complicated to see whether they have features to which she can project. A mother with eating problems who obsess over the weight of her daughter is preparing. The daughter does not know this because she probably internalized an absurdly slim vision of women's weight, and therefore supports the projection of her mother.

If the narcissist advises the daughter to consume too much, work out harder, or wear incredibly big garments, the daughter insists on it, even though it is not real. Still, though, she designs as though it makes little sense whatsoever. This is because she feels shameful and has to impose that on her baby boy, and the screening is also a blue assault. For starters, she makes an outrageous request and, at times, declines to let her go. She is angry that they are resisting and screams that they can talk about it and are no longer hysterical after they have cooled down.

They aren't at all hysterical; she is, but his denial made her feel the guilt that should have prevented her from making shameless statements. That's unacceptable. This is intolerable. She should put the embarrassment upon kids and streamline response. When finished, she will reassert her disgrace and engage in her childish will by translating an unequivocal rejection into a matter of further debate.

3.1.20. Always right

She's never wrong. Regardless of what she did, she would never ever apologize for something. Instead, suppose she thinks like she is made to apologize. In that case, she sulks and shrugs, sends insulting apologies, or refuses the apology she has just provided with justifications, credentials, or self-pity. Another indication of projection is the last insulting apology.

3.1.21. Lacks sympathy

Occasionally, she can slip and tell something mischievously callous owing to this loss of sensitivity. It's not like she doesn't worry about the emotions of anyone, but she doesn't. Simply it will never happen to her to worry about their emotions. The distinguishing characteristic of a narcissist is a lack of empathy that underlies much of the other characteristics. As compared to psychopaths, narcissists recognize positive, evil, and effects and are not ordinarily criminal. She hit, so they didn't go to the ambulance. She left them in the ice until they became wretched, but not until they had hypothermia. She put them in the basement without any clothing in the dark, but just for two hours, she left them there.

3.1.22. Blame others

She would accuse him of everything that is not good with her life and for what others do or what has happened. She'll always blame him for her violence. He did that to her. If only kids haven't been too rough. They are so frustrating her that she can't think clearly. Things were complicated for her, and backtalk was driving her to the edge. This allegation is always so subtle that all they remember is that they assumed they were incorrect, and suddenly they feel guilty. After all, she knew how hard it is for her to love. She is trying to do something egregiously exploitative for them, and when she challenged screams at them so that she can't imagine that they became so egoistic over such an insignificant matter. She is also going to fault them for their response to her greedy, inhuman, and exploitative actions. She can't imagine that they are so tiny, so small and infantile that they can object to her offering her friend their favorite outfit. She figured they would be able to let someone else do something good to her.

Narcissists are practitioners at multitasking. Their manipulative mother is at the same time 1) misleading. She knows what she has done has been wrong, and she recognizes that their response is rational. 2) Manipulate. She makes him appear like a poor guy who objects to her brutality. 3) Being egoistic. She doesn't care to make him feel bad as long as she gets to her own road. 4) Blaming: She made an error, so it's their entire fault. 5) The preparation. Her little, petty and childish conduct is now theirs. 6) Putting on a compassionate drama. She's a hero, and they have let her down, who thought the best of them. 7) Prettification. She has no liability for her; they are responsible for her emotions.

3.1.23. Rule over social connections

Narcissistic mothers are like tornadoes: households are torn apart, and casualties are inflicted everywhere they strike. If the father manages the narcissist and maintains the family intact, adult siblings are usually traumatic in narcissistic mothers' households. Normally, all conversation between siblings is shallow and duties-driven or will never speak to each other. In part, these women encourage disagreement among their children because they have the influence they have. If they don't talk more than by the mother, she will dictate what everyone hears. Narcissists really enjoy the thrill and drama that they generate by messing in the lives of their children. It is easier to see people's lives erupt than soap operas, especially because they have no empathy for their suffering.

The narcissist nurtures rage, disdain, and jealousy, the most corrosive feelings, to force her children away. Any kid who stands before the narcissist promises retribution for the others because her children are still living at home. In her core for vengeance, the narcissist focuses the wrath of the brothers and sisters on the dissident with everyone participating in her reprisals. The other children trained to give in by the narcissist are upset with the troubled boy instead of with the narcissist who merits their rage.

The narcissist often utilizes favoritism and rumors to poison the relationships between her children. The mother is seen as a creature of caprice and cruelty by the scapegoat. As is common for the wealthy, the other children do not see their oppression and justify their violence. In reality, the Narcissist is always hired to take her contemptuous and legitimate stance towards the scapegoat and can proceed to administer violence with her implicit or overt approval. The scapegoat reacts with fury and equal scorn predictably. When her children go on with adult lives, the narcissist maintains that each person knows what other people do and passes on the discrediting and juicy gossip about other children, once again, in a manner that gives rise to disdain rather than sympathy (as often veiled as 'concern').

Since a narcissist has been brought up, her offspring are inclined to jealousy and taking full advantage of the chance. While she can never compliment them, she's going to crowd their successes to their sibling who doesn't do well. She would remind them of her kindness to this boy, leaving them questioning why they missed out and became irrationally upset with the chosen child instead of with the narcissist.

The end effect is a family in which almost all is triangular. The narcissist, who is the spider inside the family network, tracks all children sensibly for their knowledge to maintain their unquestioned power over the family. She transmits this to others and induces frustration that prohibits them from interacting directly and honestly. The consequence is that the only contact with the girls, just as she wishes, is through the narcissist.

3.1.24. Pathetic

She would crumble into a soggy puddle of crying holiness until faced with imminent repercussions for her own poor conduct, including wrath. It is her responsibility. She will do it right. She cannot do something right. It looks so bad. It sounds so bad what she is not doing: owning and correcting the blame for her poor behavior. It is more about her instead, as usual, and her weak, self-sufficient crying shoots away from the blame for its repercussions

AND her frustration with them. Like narcissists too much, it's just deceptive conduct. They are the wrong ones to be calm, cardiac, and unfeeling if they do not justify her unpleasant actions to make her feel stronger. If their poor mother feels too terrible."

3.2 Types of Narcissistic Mothers

So, the following six types of narcissistic mothers are recognized. A maternal parent can also be an amalgam of these types. Let's have a look over these faces

The Pretentious-Extrovert

Such a mother can be seen in the movies. She is a communal fun, liked by many, but partner and children fear her the most. She is the one who sets the stage and performs on it. She's prominent, flamboyant, entertainment, and "the center." A few people love her, but the child despises the masquerade she's performing for the world.

The Attainment-Oriented

What a kid achieves in his life is the uppermost concern of an accomplishment-oriented mother. This mom only cares about grades, colleges, and degrees. If she doesn't do what she thinks a child should do, she's deeply ashamed and may get annoyed and irritated.

The Irrational

The sick mom takes on illnesses and pain to exploit others and distract everyone to her. She hardly cares for others. If she wants to get the attention of such a mother, then only by taking care of them. These mothers use illness as an excuse to run away from their own emotions or life problems. She's sicker than a child.

The Obsessed

A maternal parent who is drug-addicted is mostly narcissistic because the obsession will speak clearly. When such a mother is less addicted, then narcissism is less extreme, but not always. They prefer a bottle or drug to a child.

The covertly selfish

She will never want others to know that she is rude and noisy to her children. She will have two faces - a public self and a private self — utterly opposite.

She can be kind and loving in public but is rude and noisy at home. The unforeseeable, contrasting messages make a child go crazy.

The Sentimental Poor

Narcissistic mothers are somewhat more pre-occupied than other mothers. This mother is to be emotionally looked after, which is not an ideal situation for a child. Because a child's emotions have not been nurtured, that child is unlikely to receive an equal level of attention that a child is looked forward to giving to a parent.

3.3 Manipulative Tactics Employed

If children are kept exposed to abusive narcissistic mothers, they carry on experience with exploitation in adolescence. The very tactics will be employed as in childhood that can still be Herculean, causing to sink in childhood fright, guilt, and panic.

Following tactics are usually employed to shatter the self-confidence of a child, which eventually have far-sighted effects.

Emotional Blackmailing

The toxic mothers appear to appeal but are really an order. If a child says no, then the pressure will increase. If they still refuse their request, then punish with passive aggression or even threatened with brutality or wreck. It is named as an emotional blackmailing

Precautionary measurement

Be conscious of privileges and boundaries. A child will have the freedom to refuse an offer, appeal, or invitation by someone who is rude. As a family member that is affected by a toxic mother's actions, he has the right to defend him. Never give in to the silent treatment or suffer the angry assaults. It is not a negotiation to not speak with them in person.

Guilt Tripping with Fear, Obligation, and Guilt

This commonly employed tactic to evoke guilt in the child to give in to her desires and demands at the cost of his basic wants and privileges.

Precautionary measurement

The remorse, embarrassment, and self-loathing that emerge from being taken advantage of by a manipulative parent are to be noted. Don't condemn for it. Reflect forward on whether or not you have something to really feel bad for. Have you deliberately caused some damage to an abusive parent? One must have the freedom to make own decisions, appreciate own interests, and have own liberty, even though a toxic or unsupportive mother opposes it. In no way, shape, or type indebted to them a reason for decisions that include job, relationship, or any children might or may not have.

Shaming

The toxic mothers shame their child to belittle as it is actually effective as research has shown that when one finds that he is defective, they are more obliged to the requests than others' demands.

Precautionary measurement

Suppose children are experiencing hallucinations linked to some span of time where a mother will bring up history as critique, accept it. During this moment, educate that this guilt should not live on and remind how far they have come. It's time to be proud of, not embarrassed

Comparison and Triangulation

The toxic mothers love to compare their children with others to diminish their self-respect. They want their scapegoats to prove their worth. This tactic makes children feeling less than others.

Precautionary measurement

Do not be scared of contrasting. Turn the topic or find a way to end the dispute immediately if the narcissistic mother begins futile, emotionally offensive complaints and hateful chatter. When getting the need to defend or describe, still don't do it.

Gas lighting

It is an insidious tool in the toolbox which is employed to distort reality and make a child toxic for calling them out. This tool is psychological exploitation with which she will turn the tables around for a child and drag him to the state of insanity. She will make him feel guilty, and thus, their bond is imbalanced. This creates doubts in the mind of the child, and he develops low self-esteem and self-confidence. He no longer trusts his own perception and imagination. This tool resembles brainwashing, interrogation and torture.

Precautionary measurement

Because of their early memories, people who were gas lighted frequently struggle from this feeling of self-doubt later in life. If you had encountered something that is harmful, log the incident and focus on defining oneself as a consequence of the experience without doing what their mother suggested.

Doing so will often work to improve their connection with themselves by learning to stand on their own two feet.

Look through everything that adults have gone through and the cycles of violence. Rather than blindly believing what parent has taught, as though it weren't false, it is necessary enough to look at what the truth is. To stop the toxic parent, fight the temptation to ignore the trauma, recalling what happened and how it happened prevents from getting abused and taken advantage of by the toxic parent.

No needs to willingly endure, defend, or cover the hurtful, abusive, and harmful actions of someone who shares DNA.

Silent Treatment

She employs silence as a tool to kill a child mentally. She is named mental murder due to the same reason. She forces a child to walk on eggshell with no objection, and he does what she desires. The flying monkeys in the family make a child ashamed of and put pressure to cut a sorry figure before his mother.

Precautionary measurement

Ignore her and let her be bored as narcissistic mothers get irritated with boredom.

3.4 Narcissistic Mother- A Family Venom

Sometimes, manipulative mothers may effectively create multiple and highly destructive relational and personal tensions within their children.

She also employs the manufactured secrets (often lies) to harm and ruin the bonds between herself and her children. She will select one boy, but a special one. She will select one boy, a special one.

Being an attractive boy, highly intellectual, or able to draw may place someone at a higher or greater risk of this psychiatric condition. Her mother has idolized this child. This child is willing to be malicious, to be rude, and to be dishonest to others. The selected infant is the ultimate embodiment of the mother's fond wishes.

The selfish parent often determines another kid to be the loser. This is usually a daughter. The purpose of the narcissistic mother's manifestation of her hidden subconscious pool of levels of self and worthlessness. This infant is a mirror of what the narcissistic mother is forcing herself to become.

3.5 Confuse Children-Wearing Two Masks

Narcissistic mothers have many faces but are categorized into two on the basis of environment. They behave differently at home and in public.

Narcissistic mothers are believed to be very selfish and high self-esteem, but inside, they are not. They are unsure and need affection and appreciation.

In public, they behave as charming and entertaining being as this elevates their confidence. To be the center of attraction is their main motto. The topic of their discussion is usually the golden child in public. They take the credit for their success and show off the nurturance. While at home, they are the opposite of this. The real avatar of a narcissistic mother. They insult their child at all levels and shatter his confidence, especially scapegoats. This makes them feel right with no guilt. This gives them a sense of supreme power and satisfies their ego. If a child says yes to all her desires, he is living in a caged-paradise. Otherwise, the same home becomes hell for him. She treats him with all tactics. A child to live in an eggshell, and if one tries to break that eggshell, this puts her in rage. This develops tension in the home, and the child is blamed for all this mess.

3.6 Why Narcissistic Mothers Have Children

The narcissistic mother has children that she does not have for the same reason as others. She does so because she wants to meet her wants and desires to be fulfilled. Narcissistic moms have a special position in hell. By holding her head in the oven while her two little children slept in the same apartment, Ms. Plath indulged in the supreme selfish act of committing suicide. How thoughtful it was to lock towels in their rooms so that the fumes didn't kill them either. In order to remember her, she needed someone to survive on.

For the same purposes, as we do, narcissistic mothers have no offspring. They're not looking forward to the birth of a child, and they can't wait to see what they're going to be like, what kind of personality they're going to get or who they're going to become. No, they have children purely for one cause:

More mirrors. They have kids who support them unconditionally, not the other way around. They have kids and do something for them. They have kids to reflect on their fake pictures. They have to use, manipulate and monitor kids.

The roles of a mom are not seen as the greatest gift in life. It's a responsibility they didn't expect. They presumed that they created a little "mini-me'." They didn't take into account the reality that these spiteful, ungrateful (in their minds) little beings appear to cultivate their own personalities and wills

Sometime between age 2. As well as the rest of us, that's the best part of becoming a mom-watching our children evolve into more independent, confident, free-thinking humans. Any step is, for the narcissistic mother, a complete act of betrayal.

Kids have openly voicing feelings. This annoying practice is squashed as rapidly as possible, as emotions cannot be accepted by narcissists.

Such parents end up resenting all the work of raising a child without needing them before they excel, achieve something, or even show them their false portrait. They were hurt by youngsters, taking precious time away from their own agendas. Those who don't like having to shop for the clothes of their children, prepare meals for them, do their washing, plan for daycare, partake in activities, drive them to the residences of parents, and have birthday parties, pay for higher education, or protect them from abuse.

They'll smother and over-protect their kids under the guise they're taking care of. They would not have details about menstruation, personal hygiene (makeup, hairstyles, shaving, etc.), budgeting resources, and dating. All this helps to hold her kids under her thumb as long as possible. If they're ill-informed and over-protected, they won't feel ready to evolve or step away from her.

They also had their children used as workers. As early as possible, they will delegate all household duties. And as quickly as possible, they will work on caring for their personal belongings and garments. The older children became responsible for the younger children. It would never be enough or be treated well enough; no matter how many responsibilities her children play. They expect perfection and continuously warn their children that this quality will not be achieved.

They teach their kids to think they're the perfect mum. Any evidence is to be held hidden at all times. They'll act differently with their children

Public than at home. They would vehemently denounce their misconduct and most definitely accuse their children, changing history entirely.

Narcissistic mothers don't avoid becoming narcissists as they become teenagers. They'll play with each other's siblings. They equate siblings. They'll refer to each other's siblings. If they have one problem, they'll speak about it with others.

While they brag regarding them, they are jealous of their offspring's successes ('see how great our children turned out'). They will make snide comments if they think one of their adult children has a successful relationship, house, job, etc. They are excited, and they believe like somewhere, one of their adult children has lost (although they never inform anyone about these "failures," they are badly reflected). When needed, they are more than happy to assist as it makes them look good, and there is an added bonus to earn favors. To question a narcissistic mother is like giving the devil your soul.

Such parents take a childhood, identities, and prospective healthy marriages of infants. If their kids want to, they will continue to rob and eat their children's lives as long as they live. Recognizing why your mom never loved you without punishing yourself is painfully complicated and traumatic. She raised you to blame yourself for everything. Yet to ensure that this debilitating illness is not reinforced generation after generation, where it rightly belongs, you must blame it.

These symptoms can vary from the person wanting her feelings to be managed to that of being told that a child will ameliorate their lonely evening, hopes that she will be bonded to her husband by giving birth to a child, or even wish illusions of a second chance at life and so on.

Mothers who exhibit this symptom will give unrealistic and grandiose ideas to children. If a child will not complete her desires, wants, or dreams, then there will be a child's withdrawal or a critical, harsh, or manipulative attitude towards a child. Although the boy at times is demanding and interruptive, he does not deserve to be chastised for this, because as an imperfect being, he has the ultimate right to make his needs become a reality.

Her love is tumultuous and may be in flux. The woman views her children with different expectations. Below, there are descriptions of the three roles the sons and daughters of Narcissistic mothers will be playing.

The Lost child

This is a role that entails a great deal of neglect/ ignorance as she was not just simply aware of or interested in a child's needs. The child feels like he is not lovable and unworthy and was not treated as such.

Scapegoat Child

The role of his mother in his life causes him to never understand the good he can do. By helping a child through criticism, the mother is able to give those positive thoughts and emotions that carry more value to a child. Those accomplishments will amount to no praise to her and will bring him down into pieces of his self-confidence that arises from them.

Chosen/ Hero or Golden child

He is the opposite of the scapegoat. He is seen as a god and idealized by his toxic mother. But it was like this that he led his whole life as a victim to a toxic mother in an eggshell from which she gifted him nothing beautiful that gets lost.

3.7 Why Don't Narcissistic Mothers Change

Narcissistic mothers are known to blame their children and even the people serving them within their households for the consequences that are left unfulfilled. Friends and family members are the ones to point out the extreme oddity of the mother's behavior and to act as a voice for recommending therapy. Contrary to what most people may think, a narcissist will not seek any type of help.

Often people around toxic mothers passively suffer from precisely what they believe is the parent. Thus, it is highly unlikely that a narcissistic mother sought treatment to improve her narcissistic traits. Rather, she'd like to put her child in a therapeutic environment in the hopes that he may become an easier-to-deal-with.

Self-absorption by the narcissist causes the most suffering for the family. The narcissist does not feel it personally because they believe they are causing the victim blame.

Attitude is just attitude (though quite the opposite). People who are paranoid tend to blame everyone else for their problems. Something one had to do as a child was to essentially please his mother, so he had a place to stay for the night.

We have a modern incarnation of a disorder named Narcissistic Personality Disorder, characterized by exaggerated feelings of self-importance, fantasies of success, power and physical attractiveness that one may or may not possess a constant need for appreciation and admiration, and obsessive self-interest.

This disorder is a form of narcissism, represented in different behaviors by a narcissistic mother who may not be aware of how she is interacting with her child.

3.8 Narcissistic Mothers - Divorcing

It is the erotic aspect of the marriage system itself that accounts for divorce-initiating women. Of course, the filing of a divorce does not imply that this party plans to end up in front of a judge; a person can even file first as a jump-start negotiating strategy.

Wants to win

While there are no true "winners" in divorce, with luck, there is an equal separation of obligations and properties, which is not the opinion of the narcissist. Irrespective of the truth, she is likely to see herself as a suspect and has no hope of talking till the court decides, so one should forget about dialogue or arbitration. The only purpose is to be proved right, and the narcissist can do anything it takes to make it possible.

Plays Game

Studies demonstrate that this is the behavioral trend of the narcissistic mother, retaining dominance and advantage while holding others out of control. She would not adjust just as others are heading to court. The first line of protection would be cheating the system because it would be easy to game the family court system. This is particularly dangerous when the extraverted, charming type with a lot of money to burn is their narcissistic ex. This is also an effort to bring them down.

No sympathy

One of the hallmarks of extreme narcissism is diminished sensitivity, and what this translates into here is the utter neglect by the narcissist of how others, including her partner and, most specifically, children, maybe harmed by gameplay or other activities. Actually, when the emphasis is entirely on her, it does not happen to the narcissist; nothing really even exists but fulfilling specific wishes and desires.

Unfortunately, in difficult circumstances such as divorce, what holds most of us fairly straight and clear and helps to hold us out of court is our concern for other individuals, how they may be influenced or harmed, what they may think of our actions, and how our potential relationships may be affected. Ok, not the narcissist. He, the husband, would presumably engage in what security strategists refer to as a scorched-earth strategy, leaving little in his or her path. Unfortunately, this also affects the offspring of the couple, who become helpless puppets in the narcissist's strategizing. The gender of the narcissist, as mentioned below, really comes into the equation here, especially where there is no compromise on custody or child care.

She powers court

Narcissists need to remain in self-regulating marriages, and they can experience an exciting rush of dominance and influence by pushing them into the courts. When he was actually let go by the narcissist, she would have to find someone else to meet the need. Sadly, this also suggests that the narcissistic mother does not care how long the method takes, which is shocking but real. Again, most individuals prefer to put behind them the unpleasantness and tension of divorce and all the associated negotiations and give-and-take; that's just not true of the narcissistic mother, which makes it so much tougher to go up against one. It's a way of remaining connected. It is better to be his enemy than in his eyes to become nobody.

She wants trophy

The narcissist wants a symbolic prize to show that, and the best way to do it is for him to fold the tents and go out. It's not enough that he might tell that he or she prevailed. Besting most persons helps the narcissist feel comfortable, and it is also fought as a battle of attrition to proceed to arbitration.

Why the narcissistic mother transforms the meaning of divorce?

The probability is that, because of her reluctance to negotiate conditions on some fair basis, she has wound up in custody. It will potentially make her more relaxed to go to court and have a judge rule because it suggests that she does not have to take responsibility for the decision, even if it is not favorable. That seems counterintuitive, but the narcissist doesn't want to voluntarily give up something, and the legal system promises that it won't be her fault, win or lose.

In addition, it is possible that the phase would include:

The solution to obstruction

Family court hearings will take a lot of time depending on the state she resides in, and the narcissistic mother can instruct her solicitor to use up as much of it as necessary. Be prepared to submit plenty of motions, demands for extra time and delays, "emergencies," and the like. Regardless of whether one of them is the complainant, in both his and her filings, the narcissistic mother would be the self-described perpetrator, and the marriage revisited and retold. The point is that even though it challenges credulity, the narcissist just assumes his or her facts. Narcissists will not be reluctant to lie.

Deny arbitration or settlement

Again, time is an arrow in the quiver of the narcissist because she already understands that the longer the procedure lasts, the better it would be to control and pressure him. She depends on that. A narcissistic mother is a game player by design. There are patterns in settlement negotiations to deal with a narcissist. She does not respond to all facets of the agreement in such a manner that there are still negotiating chips to be used to interrupt the discussion or to resume anew from the beginning, and they do not respond to the problems raised. Do not anticipate good faith deals at all.

"They lack the ability to negotiate towards a middle ground; even when the facts and circumstances have changed, they will probably continue to state the same position over and over again.

Make the expenses run-up

Yeah, in most instances, money is used as a bludgeon. Whether, in reality, she wants to compensate his counsel in the end, the narcissist most definitely views it as a reasonable cost.

3.9 If Narcissistic mothers become Mother-in-law

Women who marry the caring man with a selfish mother must be trained. They may not have realized before they encountered their son's partner that this lady was determined to rule her life and make them unhappy. Many of these authoritarian moms are bonded internally with their babies. It began when the kid was really young. In certain situations, the mother will replace her son with her partner, who will become a footnote in her life. As her golden child agrees to wed, the alarm goes off.

The narcissistic mother-in-law sabotages her and talks to her in rather harsh words. She seems superficial. She's after our capital, eventually. These comments are conveyed to other relatives in a persuasive manner that pushes them against the newly-married daughter-in-law. The Narcissistic mother-in-law puts into its objective, the complete power of its ruthlessness and treachery, to ruin this marriage. This functions in several situations. The woman gives up. She was alone, degraded, misled about, and drawn into any imaginable texture of dirt. Narcissistic mother-in-law, insecure enough to call their daughter-in-law's office to talk about outrageous lies against her. What these risky, deeply troubled dysfunctional mothers may do and bring through is amazing.

Daughters-in-law frequently tolerate the shower of violence. They get sleepy, tired, depressed, and nervous. As a consequence of this extreme degree of violence, some of them experience PTSD.

The son has to choose between the disturbed fusion of his mother and his partner. If the son can't individualize from his toxic mother, there is no choice but to divorce. In certain instances, the husband wakes up and discovers that his affection for his wife and his wife becomes a different entity from his pathologically possessive mother. She does not condemn herself if she has made repeated attempts to bring peace and is mindful that she is coping with a classic narcissistic mother. The daughter-in-law should not be regretful. Honor and self-respect.

Features Displayed

If she has displayed all of the following features, they can recognize why daughter-in-law have a narcissistic mother-in-law:

1. Being so interested in her life and the life of her partner.
2. The two of them are still blamed for no reason.
3. Taking repeated visits without excuse to their place.
4. To always play the victim's part and to behave innocently.
5. She still asserts her acts and defends them.
6. It is misleading, challenging, and commanding.
7. In nearly every case, it's tough to change.

To deal with Narcissistic Mother-in-law

However, as complicated and difficult as it may sound to cope with a narcissistic mother-in-law, there are certain avenues that DIL can deal with them successfully, and some of the ways are as follows:

1. *Set limits*

Since discovering that she has a narcissistic mother-in-law, the first, only, and most critical thing to do is to create healthy boundaries. The limitations can be both physical as well as emotional. The boundaries or limitations may include how much time she should spend with her in-laws, how much she can chat on the phone with each other, how much data she can exchange with in-laws, and much more. Marital life can only be held private and discussed with the partner, so make sure she does not disclose any aspect of her marriage and friendship with a shallow mother-in-law. Narcissistic personalities, while they can look compassionate, concerned, and helpful, are always good performers, and as such, they should not be trusted. This would discourage her from meddling in her family life efficiently. One point to bear in mind when establishing limitations, though, is to guarantee that her significant partner is still mindful of the limits so that she can work things out together.

2. *Caring Partner*

It is complicated enough, to start with, to contend with a narcissistic mother-in-law, and this would definitely be the same situation with her partner. It can be such a challenge for the kid to have a parent that has Narcissistic Personality Disorder. As such, she can make sure that her partner receives all the help she can get and even give words of affirmation. Likewise, by speaking up about her issues and the challenges she faces with her Narcissistic Mother-in-law, she will also turn to her husband for help. Talking with each other would allow both of them to better appreciate each other and help them better deal successfully with their mother-in-law.

3. *Dealing with calmness*

No matter what it is she does, all her acts and all she does will still be criticized by her narcissistic mother-in-law. She is bound to condemn the manner in which she talks, works, raises her children, etc. Bear in mind, though, that an individual with Narcissistic Personality Disorder is synonymous with this stuff. As such, make sure that she is not holding anything to heart. Keep a cool and collected demeanor as she begins tossing physical abuses at her and desert herself from those circumstances. The only thing that can add fuel to the fire is to react to her, and she will get more enraged. In addition, any chance she has to tell that DILs are not good enough for her family can be exploited by her narcissistic mother-in-law. She may still find numerous reasons to accuse her of whatever she says or whatever she does. Therefore, it is critical that she always communicate with her narcissistic mother-in-law in a cool, composed, and peaceful manner. She would feel neglected when they do not fall into her pit and that could effectively deter her from utilizing her old ways.

4. *Become in charge of emotions*

A narcissistic mother-in-law is sure to say a number of stuffs that might drive her to the edge of her seat. Letting go of her emotions and lashing out, though, would do more damage than good, and this will give her more justification to quarrel with her narcissistic mother-in-law. As such, it is crucial that she is in full control of her feelings. The idea that she would be packed with a bag of mixed feelings that will contain rage, fear, annoyance, sorrow, etc., is not denied. It is then important for her to let them out, and by mental or physical exercises, she will free them. She can learn and use the abilities of anger management, practice meditation, conduct exercises, etc. When she gets her thoughts under balance and control, it will become so much simpler to communicate with and accept her mother-in-law.

Chapter 4: Narcissistic Mothers Manipulate and Damage Their Sons

4.1 Importance of Mother-Son Relationship

Sons are influenced by their mother, that the way they manners in adulthood is credited to their association with their mother. A child is only understood by his mother. From the time a boy is born until his adulthood, a boy develops a strong bond with his mother. And this bond is vital for the overall physical and mental health of the kid. In the following ways, she has an impact on his life:

4.1.1. Brilliance

Sons living with her from a young age will have a higher likelihood of being emotionally secure, which will influence them to have fewer cognitive problems. The strong relationship between them results in self-confidence. The research found that lack of a close mother-son relationship could be linked to later aggression or a tendency to avoid close relationships.

4.1.2. Hercules

When a child is loved by his mother, he becomes brave. The research also found that the closer a she is to her child, the less arrogant and lazy a child will tend to be.

4.1.3. Good at school

An attentive mother makes her son succeed in his academics. She also maintains his emotional equilibrium, which is necessary for mental development.

4.1.4. Keep manners

Intellect is taught by the mother and is later learned by the son. While living with classmates and peers, he learns self-reliance.

4.1.5. Respects women

It's important to have a strong association with the mother. He will develop manners to give regards to women in general because he has fewer tendencies to see women as inferior.

4.1.6. Less risky behavior

Boys who are close to their mothers behave less-risky. Positive parent-child relationships reduce the impact of friend's pressure. The mother will have an eye on his negative vibes like smoking, drugs, alcohol, etc.

4.1.7. Likely to become successful

Being involved in her son's education and life helps him become above all others in professional and personal life. She is his friend, mentor, philosopher and guides him.

4.1.8. Improves communication

By open communication, a mother becomes her son's confidante. She is comfortable talking to her son, no matter what age he is. This makes the sons feel comfortable communicating.

Fathers are not as visible as mothers are in showing love for their children. But, as a child develops, the expression of love shifts.

4.2 Mother-Son Bond Evolves Over Years

The mother takes care of a child in the early years of his life. The moment a patient and their son or daughter is born is the moment they physically and emotionally link, at least for the first time. The child comes to rely on her in almost every aspect of their life, and this tight connection with her helps to form a strong bond. Here are the three different phases of this boy's life, focusing on what happens during each phase.

Early childhood

The baby and mother's bond is formed inside the womb. As early bonding is established, a child begins to take in the emotions of the parents, and as the parenting continues, a child takes in more and more responsibility. Studies have observed that if a mother has a positive relationship with her son, then a child will develop good mental health. As his mother enlists his grandparents' help to take care of him, he slowly learns to believe and secure.

Teenage

It is a turmoil stage in the life of boys, and it's important for them to face both internal and external changes during a boy's development. A mother helps her son endure the difficult teenage years. In the adolescent years, boys are at the height of their peer pressure to experiment with cigarette and alcohol use.

When she talks honestly with her son, it establishes a basis for the boy to distinguish between what is right and what is wrong. An affectionate mother is a source of stability and guidance for the boy.

These boys like to be considered adults/ mature men. When she generally asks for advice from a son or encourages him to participate in a family discussion, they feel appreciated. There is also a benefit in his self-worth and self-confidence.

Adulthood

The stage when she gives useful advice to her son. While mothers are known to be sentimental in nature, they also tend to be very tough. She encourages her sons to achieve their careers and value independence. She encourages her sons to pursue their interests and dreams.

With a good relationship with his mother, he learns a lot in his relationship with his wife as well. A man who respects her also respects his spouse. Peaceful marriages have a number of benefits, such as a healthy mother-child association.

It is important for the mother to care about and stand by her son as he grows into manhood (a form of manhood that beings have rather than humans). The mother is only protecting him from the ills of society and bad company.

4.3 Son of Narcissistic Mothers

When a son has a narcissistic mother, his life faces ups and downs as narcissistic mothers' son develops the crippled quality of independence, self-respect, and relationships with women.

Narcissistic mothers lack sympathy and the ability to nurture their children. They crush the individuality of a son, but as an extension of themselves. They consider themselves the center of attraction and manipulate the son's love to win others' affection. They punish him with brutality, chilliness, or concealing. Lack of confidence drives their desiring needs for respect and honor.

4.4 Bond of Son and Narcissistic Mother

They are possessed by sons. Their lives are lives that are never their own.

Their mouths speak through them. They are never free from the mother of a narcissist. Even when she is emotionally gone, she is still there. The son of

This woman who loves him has been internalized by this selfish mother.

He has been her emotional possession for his entire psychological possession in several ways. She referred to him as "her prince." For much of his life, his friendship and was deeply ambivalent regarding

She was continuously meddling. The delusional mother is building her son's fake self. She determines who he should be.

Whether he is the golden boy, he can do no wrong. It does not grow a conscience, takes advantage of people, and is implacable and ruthless.

Some narcissistic mothers have no attention to their sons, while others are over-involved. Some act aggressively, while others act caringly. Here are a few usual patterns

4.4.1. Neglect

Mothers who have negative feelings towards motherhood might neglect their son, yet they will often publicly judge their son for being too needy or childlike. As they are themselves needy, they can't bear their own child's needs. They may want their young son to be a man or favor one child while disregarding or belittling the other. This behavior is called "parental intrusiveness" or "parental favoritism."

4.4.2. Tangled

Enmeshed mothers are narcissistic. Mothers use their sons for narcissistic supply. A mother may appear self-reliant and maybe sentimental and nurture an interconnection with the son. She may rely on her son for emotional support, listening, and being a companion. In adolescence, she may turn to him for financial and legal advice.

She is all about using and exploiting him to provide her attention, affection, and fulfillment. She reinforces his dependency, making him feel valued. However, it's only to her delight. Her flooded involvement hides her toxic parenting. By manipulating him with rage, guilt, self-pity, and she makes him obliged to do what she wants.

4.4.3. Utopian Relation and Judgment

Narcissistic mothers idealize their young son. They nurture his self-reliance and self-worth. When he matures and challenges her control, she tries to rid him of his individuality. She strengthens her ego by bragging about her son. However, at home, she's critical. He may become out of sorts and act in a child-like way to be acknowledged by his parents. His fall can be disturbing. If a child is born, he loses specialness, and sibling rivalry can be extreme.

4.4.4. Triangulation

Narcissistic mothers may manipulate their son as a friend or confidant. Children are good subjects for study as they utopianism their parents and are easy to control. It is more problematic for a son if the father is angry, violent, or using drugs. The son turns to addictions or develops a close relationship with his mother in order to feel better.

4.4.5. Jealousy and Control

When a narcissistic mother realizes her son has made a female friend, she may compete with the new girl, like an angry mother is jealous of a beautiful daughter. This patient is so egotistical, and she doesn't think anyone is good enough for her. He puts her in the number one position. The woman might continue to undermine and manipulate his intimate relationships over time. Her son will be helpless and guilt-ridden because he will be caught in the middle of his mother's conflicts with his father. There is a good possibility that he feels guilty about his actions.

4.5 Impairment to Son of Narcissistic Mother

Sons of narcissistic mothers are not loved on the basis of their self-worth. Love is not given unconditionally. They are not trying to understand their son's unique, true self. When the sun catches up with her, his monetary value increases significantly. Pressure an individual into a chosen profession and the kind of lifestyle they want.

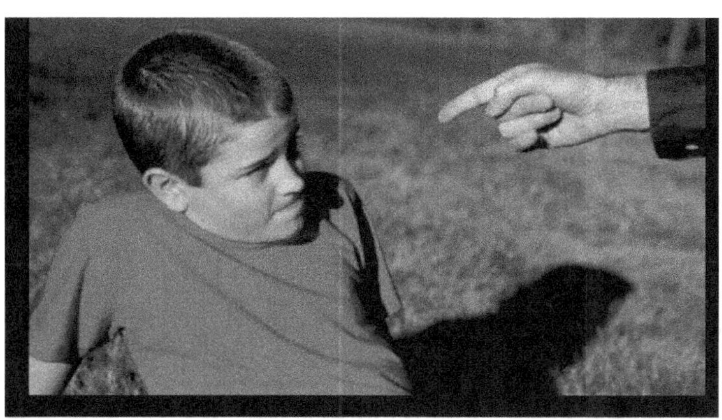

4.5.1. Interdependent

If sons are successful, they're the most likely to grow up feeling interdependent. Privacy rights have never been upheld. Their sense of self-respect and self-reliance has been damaged by verbal abuse and a lack of nurturing. They learned to accommodate their mother to avoid conflict by negating their desires, emotions, and privileges. Denial causes problems in adulthood. They cannot articulate what they want and how they feel. They may sacrifice and feel unworthy without people authentication. The father did not resist his wife's assault on children; the father failed to model how to set boundaries. As a result, sons can feel used and resentful towards their mothers.

4.5.2. Confidentiality issues

A son does not express his needs and wants to seek help from their mother as he feels insecure; the same is felt in adult intimate relationships. Being exploited and sentimentally ignored, he has become worried that his partner will abandon him. His mother being enmeshed with him, so now he fears being enmeshed with a confidant. As a consequence, he will avoid intimacy, triggering his partner's demand for increased intimacy, which enhances his anxieties and defenses.

4.5.3. Resentment

When the son feels controlled or exploited, there is a tendency for him to abhor his mother. Often other women are affected. He reacts to females with deference, resistance, or hostility. Some men are aggressive and distrustful. Merely being male is no guarantee of becoming manipulative. They constantly seek to accommodate, lie, and passively refuse appeals of their partner like they were their mother's requests. Their spouse may eventually become like their mother if they keep acting like their mother. Resentful and fearful of intimacy, their parents might have made them deprived of loyalty and honesty.

4.5.4. Repetition

The children of narcissists may also suffer from this disorder. The Son of a narcissistic mother is more likely to be narcissistic as she idealizes him than compete with a daughter.

Sons may exhibit their mothers' relationships with stressful or abusive women. Partnerships with older women can be formed with narcissistic personalities, addicts, or borderline personalities. It is difficult for them to run away from their partner and will assume the role of caregiver.

A son has to accept his mother's personality disorder, his rage against her, and his loss in order to heal. At some point, a child must accept his parents, even if he doesn't like or love them. In the current situation, he must acknowledge his value, set boundaries with his narcissistic mother, learn to say no to others, and accept his emotions and wants.

4.6 Do Sons become Narcissistic-men

Narcissism is where one has an undue appreciation and fanciful views about oneself. Mothers with narcissistic personality disorder appear to be arrogant, insecure, and concerned with becoming possibly the best. These mothers are often very unpleasant to deal with, or they have a bad relationship with others. The inflated air added on top of the usual ego prohibits individuals from sustaining a stable, long-term partnership. Adults who become parents see their children as a mirror of them, as their own personal model. Parents try to drive their children towards achievement in the areas of life they find most important. Narcissists can appreciate getting the power of something and even have the desire to stay in control.

Children who are born to narcissistic parents are at a greater risk of being narcissistic themselves. However, it has been observed that sons raised by narcissistic mothers are at a greater risk of being narcissistic themselves. Thus, it all depends on the prettification. Their mothers stand as role models by showing them how to act and how to talk, rendering them accountable for not just their minds but also for actions. Birds of a feather flock together that is both son and mother are narcissistic, and therefore like and understand each other.

Looking at the surface, the parent might look like she is validating her son, but a deeper look will show she is doing just the opposite. At the height of their pride, she places him on a plinth to make him feel like he is the greatest. As a boy, the son would feel more secure about him, so he can quickly get puffed up. However, having him on such a plinth will make it harder for him to tolerate falling down.

He will remain focused on this strategy because he feels better about his plan to show himself today. However, at some stage, his mother would become frustrated with him leading him to experience a great deal of pain. Son will try more and more to impress his mother because she has very high expectations and will continue to struggle to do so because it is not feasible to consistently satisfy an egomaniac. She will start to hate the boy, and the son will eventually begin to experience anger as well.

Usually, he would also continue to despise her since he is no longer getting the admiration he's been used to, and his ego is not receiving the encouragement that he is used to. He finds a way for him to inflate his own self-worth by getting stuck on with means that resist outside criticism. He pays attention to take control of his own ego. As said above, the son grows up to be a guy who idealizes himself, places his own interests first, and feels that he is entitled to everything. As a consequence of it all, he lacks the capacity to make peace, concentrating instead on his own emotions and desires and, in doing so, denies the emotions and desires of others. In fact, his son is a highly vulnerable individual who tries out methods of suppressing his true terror.

Instead of the mother-son partnership, several other forms of partnerships may also be influenced. Still, a boy of a narcissistic mother grows up to be a narcissist; it is mainly attributable to nature. One factor that is crucial is the connection between parents and children. Today, the interactions between children and their parents are very important. Therefore, it is important to understand the effects on children from the form of attachment the parents give.

4.7 To Fix A Broken Mother-Son Bond

It's not convenient for men to conquer suffering. They have more issues than women when voicing their emotions and are more self-censoring and even harsher on themselves. Men are less forgiving of flaws and less patient with the healing method.

Maternal manipulative violence is common among men. They experience a lifetime of devastating physical suffering without support.

The children of narcissistic mothers have a vacuum within which their mother's affection, promotion, acceptance, and affirmation would have filled. They miss the triumphant feeling and faith in the achievement of Freud's words, "When a man has been the undisputed darling of his mother, he retains the triumphant feeling, the trust in the success that often brings true success to him."

As adults, these men aspire for achievement and prosperity, but nothing they do is ever pleasing without the cornerstone of their mother's affection.

Narcissistic women, like their children, assign their son's childhood tasks. All three positions are similarly violent, although in differing forms.

There's still a golden kid, an evil boy, and even an unseen boy. If only one child is present, he will perform a number of roles. Roles can be changed, but only one golden kid can be changed at a time.

4.7.1. Self-help

f a relationship is broken, the best thing to do is to help oneself. Don't let the past hold one back; take charge of the future by making the right choices today.

4.7.2. Seek counseling

Seek the advice of a counselor or therapist and disclose worries with them. Discuss concerns with a third party who can offer an objective and good solution to the problem.

4.7.3. Take responsibility

Take responsibility for everything that has gone wrong, and let your son know that he was not at fault and don't hold any grudges against him.

4.7.4. Talk it out

Break the ice and start a conversation with your son or mother. Express love to them and tell them how much she cares about them. So show son/mother the affection and concern.

4.7.5. Be patient

A little of the right things can go a long way. Give son some time to accept the truth and reality. A calm mind helps in setting things in perspective. He will realize that he Is trying to fix Ihe bond.

4.8 When Son of Narcissistic Mother Marries

t may be toxic for a boy's mental well-being to have a manipulative mother, which is especially acute in how he communicates with women as an adult. Never have these sons encountered true affection that is not transactional. It would also be even more challenging for them to open up and to develop relational intimacy. Their partnerships would be superficial and focused on the relational vacuum left by the mother being fulfilled.

Narcissistic women, out of envy and fear of destroying their supplies, are even more prone to undermine their son's relationships. Narcissistic mothers will point out their son's future girlfriend's defects during a partnership's dating process. The son may not want to be trapped between a disapproving mother and his current girlfriend, so he's going to break the engagement and endure short-term and insubstantial flings down a loop.

This is to say less about the difficulties of living with a narcissistic mother-in-law. Narcissistic rules will aim to separate their offspring in order to assert control over their son or daughter-in-law.

The child may often understand the trauma that is caused but sometimes remains ignorant or feel too helpless to question the adult. If grandchildren are involved, and the narcissistic mother will use them to shame her son and his partner, the problem becomes much more difficult.

Chapter 5: Will Daughter Ever Be Good Enough - Toxic Mother's Corrosive Envoy

5.1 Importance of Mother-Daughter Relationship.

It has been found that the relationship between the mother and her daughter is stronger than the relationship between two random individuals. And this is one relationship that is important in helping a girl carve out every other relationship she has in life. Because the relationship is important for everyone, it is very valuable.

It will change in time. There are always a lot of problems and issues during the time. That's usually because of the generational differences. Even mothers will use certain measures to protect their daughters. And they correct their daughters. There's a saying, "Like mother, like daughter."

The relationship between mothers and daughters varies from one to another. Some mother-daughter relationships can be tense from the very beginning, while other relationships take a difficult path when the daughter grows up. Any type of undesirable behavior between a mother and a daughter could impact the mother-daughter relationship.

This healthy association impacts in the following ways:

5.1.1. No guilt

They both do not guilt/shame each other. They never do any act at the cost of the dignity of each other. Their bond is the true depiction of mutual trust. Placing an excessive amount of emphasis on the other party's recent past errors will only damage the relationship. People avoid being around those who call themselves bad. In order to make the best out of the relationship, focus on getting past the pain and finish "guilt speech" from this association.

5.1.2. Valuable company

They make their time worthy of spending together. Irrespective of how close a mother-daughter relationship is, there have to be certain boundaries. Both can be best friends, but there have to be healthy boundaries. This not only helps in improving the bond but also maintains a respectful relationship.

5.1.3. Never change

They accept each other the way they are. The mother and daughter are two different individuals having different perceptions. They both accept each other with no offense. Deals within a healthy association are not based on seeking to change each other. Each person accepts the other for who they are. If a mother wishes her daughter and a younger child were more alike, we should let that go. If she tries to watch out for her mother and change her into a more acceptable figure, this is not healthy. Respect one another authenticity. People focus on the positive while ignoring negative messages. If they do not match expectations, focus on the most positive aspects of what they have to offer. Focus on how the relationship is made strong.

5.1.4. Ignore Differences

They do not ignore differences but have a table talk to come to the point of mutual understanding. It's only natural to have tension in this association. Mother and Daughter must understand each other and agree or disagree. Ignoring problems will only create bigger problems coming up. This enables the emotional deformation of said anger. The dam breaks, and blood will spill onto the floor. Exert effort in conflict, but do so in a constructive way. Never let one another down in a way that demeans or disrespects another. Make both sides of the argument comprehensible and provide the relevant evidence. Be intellectually honest and realize that to have opposing points of view, and still like one another, anyway.

5.1.5. Active-listeners

They reciprocate their relationship and are very good active-listeners depicting a healthy association that is like a two-way street. Most of the misunderstandings occur due to no communication at all. Mother and daughter should be open to having healthy and honest communication.

5.1.6. Independent and strong

Both are independent to take decisions as the mother made her daughter confident enough to take the right decision with dignity and pride. She never considers her mother a life-boat. It is necessary for both to comfort each other when there are severe problems. It has benefits and drawbacks too. If a mother always helps her child, the bond between the mother and daughter will not be strong. Mothers should assist their daughters to fail at times, as it helps to develop and improve. Although this relationship is delicate, the mother should not poke her nose when the daughter is trying to deal with a problem. This strategy makes the daughter strong and worthy.

5.2 Trust Entails Mother-daughter bonding

Trust is important in a relationship for mutual support between daughters and mothers. Trust is often a challenge during maturity, but they should work hard to win their trust as they mature. Mothers must be open and honest with their daughters. Keep promises they make to her.

Both individuals have to be loyal to one another, even if it is painful. Women, even after they are grown up, should still tell their mothers the truth.

Both can flourish in an open and trustworthy relationship.

Set boundaries to avoid entrapment. It is the duty of the mother to set limits, and the daughter must be abiding by these limits and resolve conflicts through table-talk.

Space is needed once a daughter leaves the nest. A daughter may need to set boundaries when she visits her mother and what she says to her mother on the phone. It is important that mother and daughter have their own boundaries and be allowed to be themselves.

Healthy relationships involve a form of communication. It is essential to regard respect even when disagreeing. Insults against either mother or daughter should be avoided.

Mothers and daughters have positions of great importance in each other's lives.

If one wants to maintain a good mother-daughter relationship, be careful in interactions. Keep communicating openly. One another can be the best.

Even if arguing, continue telling each other how much you love each other and show that to one another.

5.3 Daughters of the Narcissistic Mother

Narcissistic mothers may tend to the physical needs of their daughters but neglect to nurture their emotions. Her daughter doesn't know what she truly wants but longs for the love and warmth that she may experience with friends or relatives or witness in other mother-daughter relationships. Daughters of narcissistic mothers often get into relationships with narcissists. These people may seem wonderful at the start. Attentive, caring, sensitive, generous, but slowly they come to the realization that they want to control and dominate them, subtly but insidiously, just like dear old mom. Remember, narcissists, are initially charming. The daughters of narcissistic mothers have a sense of remorse and indebtedness, being worthless human, translating frustration like the angry conviction that she is lying about herself and being inept and losing trust. She encounters a situation where she feels she starts and stops, where the borders become blurred. She may have limited contact with others and worried about life or nervous about something.

Their attention is flattering, especially if they have been starved of affection and attunement in the past. If raised by a narcissist, then likely to be much more vulnerable because the daughter just doesn't have that sense of inner stability and security. Nor did she understand how healthy relationships work. Daughters of narcissistic mothers are very vulnerable to the seductive thrill of someone who unconsciously reminds them of an abusive parent.

The traits of having a narcissistic mother are explained below.

It is common for intimate partners to return to abusive situations because it experiences like "home" to them.

5.3.1. Lack of Boundaries

Girls are more influenced by their mothers than boys and look up to them as role models. Narcissistic mothers notice their daughters as threatening and reflect on themselves. As they try to influence their children to be like them, they shape their daughters to be like them. Inwardly, they feel very upset with their daughter.

5.3.2. Narcissistic abuse

Repeated shaming and control instill feelings of insecurity. She cannot trust her own feelings and impulses, so she thinks that she is responsible for her parents' unhappiness. After severe abuse or neglect, girls may feel they are a burden on their mother and shouldn't exist. A girl won't learn to be courageous. She may be unable to remember any mistreatment later in life.

5.3.3. Toxic shame

She feels alone and unsupported by her peers. She must choose between being the "sacrificial lamb" and remaining in an unhealthy, codependent relationship. She rejects herself because she thinks her mother created her. The consequence is a perceived unbearable internalized shame for the real person. Why does the mother love herself but not her own daughter? Adding shame, guilt, and anger, a daughter's shame multiplies. She believes her mother's criticism is true, and she is bad. Her life is one of constant striving towards personal fulfillment. As she grew older, her relationships with adults became more volatile.

5.3.4. Emotional unavailability

The lack of maternal affection and tenderness results in coldness and distance. Narcissistic mothers tend to physical needs but neglect their emotional well-being. The daughter did not know what she was missing in her life, but she longed for warmth and understanding from her mother. She wants a sense of connectedness. She is unable to identify and value her emotional needs. Thus, her grief stems from her inability to provide comfort to herself. Emotional unavailability often occurs in other relationships but recurs in current relationships.

5.3.5. Control

Narcissistic mothers are myopic. They control their children's needs, feelings, and choices whenever possible, and they take failure to do so as an affront and a personal affront. Narcissistic mothers focus all of their energy on themselves or their sons and often neglect the development of their daughters.

Other mothers want their daughter to be the best version of self, but they attempt to control their daughter, degrading her in the process. Such mothers try to maintain a positive relationship with their daughter, who they view as a part of themselves. Their attention to their daughter is accompanied by their envy of her and their expectations of gratitude.

5.3.6. Competition

Narcissistic mothers who believe their daughters are "the fairest of all" criticize their daughters and compete with them for their sons' and husband's love. Mothers may deny or protect their daughters from being abused if they are abused.

5.4 Envious of their Daughters

The influence of two types of narcissism on the propensity to feel envy was also studied by a report in 2020, and they also explored how this was related to relational violence.

Their studies found that grandiose narcissists exhibited less envy than vulnerable narcissists, even if all styles continued to mentally manipulate their intimate partners. If they've ever been in a narcissistic relationship, this latter argument is not going to come as much of a surprise.

Nevertheless, they observed that envy was a big risk factor for insecure narcissists in carrying out the violence.

The motive behind the violence is also a little different, according to this report. For the standard purposes, grandiose narcissists' abuse: to seize power, retain superiority or raise their own self-esteem. They can feel envy, but for them, at least while they are in a good mood, it's not a big phenomenon.

Vulnerable narcissists, though, are a bit odd. They are especially susceptible to intimacy threats, and they get jealous quickly because of this. And, sadly, they are likely to strike out at their mate as they do. This is not the only cause of why they can become violent, but it is a catalyst.

While mother-daughter relationships, in general, are wonderful, they can be difficult to navigate so well. Both sides are responsible for these problems. The mother can be self-centered, grandiose, and rude, but she can also be absent, distant, cold, and even completely envious of her daughter.

It is difficult for some mothers to be nice, and they cause feelings of envy to persist instead of enhancing their current life or being satisfied with the phase of life they are in.

It starts to sound a lot less strange when they see it from a mom's perspective. Let's see how a mother is affected by the growth of her daughter.

5.4.1. Mothers try to be a spotlight

If mom is feeling envious, she might try to steal the attention by copying or even one-upping. Daughters cannot mention their success, accomplishments, be part of a competition, or doing shopping without, yes, a narcissistic mother. Her actions make it feel like a competition. A toxic mom who is envious cannot endure her daughter to be above her or of her level.

5.4.2. She gets bored

These mothers do not listen to their daughter, as they want to protect themselves from being exposed and will leave the daughter empty. They show their disinterest during a conversation. Egotistical mothers have a difficult time expressing their genuine joy and happiness in response to their daughter's accomplishments, so they just might try to steal comfort for themselves.

5.4.3. Backbite

She will eventually hone in on every flaw of her daughter. If the daughter made a mistake at work, she might say something at the daughter's back. If the skin breaks out, she might make unnecessary comments about it. This is meant to offend someone, and it can be truly cruel and unfair.

5.4.4. Changes looks

If her appearance begins to change suddenly, it may indicate her insecurity. Narcissistic mothers who are jealous of their daughters are sometimes seen to be behaving childishly.

This joke may be funny in the beginning but don't overlook the fact that it stems from a place of pain. They just like to have fun, while others might be trying to keep up with the young children in their households because of insecurity.

5.4.5. Overreaction

A wide variety of factors can cause someone to be triggered. If they over-react after the fight, it could mean that they are suffering from underlying jealousy. She may be ironic, annoyed, and quiet or makes personal attacks.

This can make the daughter wonder why she is acting so strangely.

5.4.6. Touchy about a bond with father

When they become envious of a father/daughter type of relationship. If she gets upset by this inside joke that, in her eyes, makes her irrelevant to her daughter. She may get upset if daughter-father spends time together. Even if the daughter has any relation with or without her confirmation, narcissistic mothers do get envious due to insecurity and grandeur.

It is the basic right of every individual in general and daughters in specific that mothers or fathers should not interfere in any of their social, personal, or business relationships.

5.4.7. Not happy with the success

If such a mother rejects success, it is because she would like to have received the same. Some mothers might get jealous of their daughters, especially when they receive the praise and recognition other kids get, such as when their daughter does well at school or has lots of friends.

An emotionally jealous mother will constantly compare herself (parts) to other people and may choose her daughter as her barometer of success.

Don't forget or hide the pain, however difficult it might be to deal with it. It does not mean the daughter has to downplay or give up on her goals or her mother's request to do so. While that may be what she serves her daughter to do when she is in a time of a negative mood, the remedy really does have a hint on her being, which she will hopefully decide to do.

5.4.8. Always judgmental

A narcissistic mother has a way of speaking to express her own insecurity. This is something one can turn a frown upside down in life. Once in a while, boundaries could be of assistance. The daughter can pick and choose what to share with the toxic mom. Daughters can even create a little distance between them.

5.4.9. No concern about daughter

One could just say toxic mom is busy, but it could mean she isn't concerned about a daughter. That means she can be envious and is keeping things from her daughter because of her own issues with the envoy. If her attention starts to wane, this will be a problem.

If everything they say is about her despite her never asking how they are or what they're up to, this may be a sign of jealousy. And since a mother is supposed to be one of a student's highest praise, it may feel embarrassing.

For personal benefit, daughters need to broaden their circle to find more people who can build them up, such as aunts and friends. To fill the role of their mom being absent, it helps to find someone else who can.

5.4.10. Considers daughter wrong

She protects her daughter by confronting her and always disagreeing with the daughter. She believes the things she does for others are a way of boosting her self-esteem. Try not to take things personally by not commenting back, or it might make things worse. Toxic Mom's use may drop off, and she'll be a little more considerate.

5.4.11. Ready to quarrel

If a toxic mom feels threatened by a relationship her daughter has with other family members, including dad, she will get jealous and try to cause trouble. She will give an exaggerated reply in a way to get attention. She wanted and objected to stupid attacks coming from these ill-wishing individuals and knows that they are simply there doing. Ask a therapist for his or her advice to have limits with toxic mothers. Also, consider cutting back contact with her. If she's determined to drag her daughter down, it may be time to ask for help.

5.5 Crippled Daughters of Narcissistic Daughters

Narcissistic mothers undermine their daughters' motivations to become self-reliant free-swinging successful adults. When the mother thinks that she should have the daughter's life, she feels envious.

When the daughter grows into puberty, she will begin to undermine her actions of love. Younger men are beginning to pay attention to these issues. It is suggested that they are sexually drawn to this young lady. The selfish mother is angry that such a thing has happened. She senses jealousy in her stomach as she attempts to contend with her daughter.

An important sign of depersonalization is when a parent has a pattern of telling lies to their children, which ultimately undermines their self-confidence.

It is common for a narcissistic mother to hold her daughter since childhood in every walk of life. There may also be a feeling of experiencing poor self-esteem.

The selfish mother supports her daughter's ability to succeed at all costs. The narcissistic mother takes the praise to her shoulders for her daughter's accomplishments. The daughter, who begins to become a voice, is a danger to the entire family.

Individualism is ridiculed. The daughter was labeled as a rebel by the narcissistic mother and was stripped of any meaningful role in the family.

5.6 An echoes Daughter of Narcissistic Mother

Not all unappreciated daughters would become echoes; her actions are formed in reaction to her mother's care for her, and certain patterns of maternal conduct are more likely to create an echo—someone who doesn't have enough healthy narcissism or self-regard—than others. The mom is narcissistically oriented. She tells her child that their role is to remain right in her good graces, continue to advocate for her affection, and appease others is above and beyond their own desires and wishes. Mothers ultimately use the daughters as extensions of her. This daughter has discovered that the only way to be effective with her mother is to be quiet.

Daughters who grow up in a dysfunctional family build a typical psychological reaction to this chaotic atmosphere, one that has an early onset in adolescence. Some of the younger girls become detached when they realize that it is uncomfortable or shameful to speak out, and they will carry on the habits of their mothers to attempt to be liked. As adults, they will begin to suppress their own beliefs and ideas as though they don't matter, and this insecurity will show out of other aspects of their lives. Mothers who have a high amount of influence over a daughter also assume that continually criticizing and questioning a girl's accomplishment can keep her from "obtaining an engorged head," becoming egoistic, arrogant, and feeling "excessively worthy of oneself"; these mothers do generate a high amount of and heavy dominant-criticism sentiment. Oppressing a daughter under the concept of being "very susceptible" or moaning out of its thoughts as a form of shielding oneself, "echoing" away one's supposed feelings is a means to shelter itself.

5.7 Complaining All the Time – Narcissistic Mothers

The selfish mom is never happy with something. Mothers who carry narcissistic traits are fascinated with an image. And if the focus daughter is only mildly overweight, her mother would regularly make sarcastic comments regarding her child's appearance.

If she has a manipulative mother, she can be highly negative. The toxic mother discovers defects in the perfect first-born daughter. A narcissistic mother displays personality traits that follow the belief that she is self-centered and that she puts herself before others. These personalities are passed through their offspring.

Narcissists have been described as "extremely self, arrogant, deceptive, devious, rapacious, and ignoring the least indication of human compassion toward others."

The majority of girls who are neglected by their abusive mothers heal. It evolves into avoidance that makes them shut out their intense feelings in order to prevent offending their mother. Some daughters step out in defiant ways, substance dependency issues, or have sex without getting married and tearing the family apart.

5.8 Damaging effects on Daughters

The powerful mother-daughter relationship is defined by the discipline and rudeness of the mother. Sometimes, narcissistic mothers make their daughters feel guilty about some of their behavior. Whether she truly cares for a child or not, she is really a selfless person.

The mother is empty of her capacity to be available for mothering. And so, the daughter may be in perpetual mourning for someone as a mother that she can never have. Years of toxic behaviors on the part of the family system will have left scars. One book to read is Motherless Daughters. It has a way of getting women to understand the effects of having missed out on mothering. Narcissistic mothers were/are never available in an emotionally supportive way that daughters need.

Exploitation also comes in the form of pretending to care deeply about a child. We can perceive that there is genuine concern about a child, but it is actually the byproduct of a guilt trip on the part of the mother. Guilt trips are the mother's attempts to manage her daughter's emotions and behavior towards her.

Control can take the form of withdrawal or indirect punishment. The manner of child-rearing shifts a child's emotional ties from the mother to others. The narcissistic mother may not respond to her children during silent treatment. They may have remained silent with a child for a long time. If the daughter wants something simple, like lunch money, her mother may send her messages which were not nice. That's a shameful thing.

Narcissistic mothers use many methods to hinder their daughters.

5.8.1. Gossiping

The narcissistic mother thrives on rumors and hearsay. It is more like a human body's they're batteries. It is the kind of behavior that some parents engage in when their kids do something terrific. Still, after the kid moves on to do something else, the parent may decide to complain and gossip to anyone who will listen about their child's abilities to their child.

The daughter is really hurt because she has to hear that her mom is very upset and angry with her. But the mother does not actually say this directly to her when the daughter is there. The mother spreads malicious gossip about the daughter behind her back.

5.8.2. Subversion

The narcissistic mother negatively influences her daughter's intimate relationships. She undermines her daughter's future. In this way, she undermines her daughter's overall happiness and growth. They'll give bad advice to the daughter, especially when she enters into intimate relationships. Narcissistic mothers believe their daughters should be married whether the daughter doesn't want to be.

5.8.3. Pessimistic Interpretation

The narcissistic mother is operating in the same way as a narcissist. They call the daughter a "whore" when she's not doing anything like that at all. The narcissistic mothers cause their daughter's emotional issues by having to enter therapy.

5.8.4. Blaming oneself

They do a great deal. They play the victim, and that makes everybody believe they are martyrs. They have been the best mom. They have been amazing mothers to their children, but their children are ungrateful, abusive, disrespectful, and do not play along. Instead, toxic mothers act like martyrs and are victimized.

5.8.5. Triangulation

They absolutely never want their daughter to be independent. In conclusion, the daughter is also suffering from the burdens of attachment. It involves isolating one or more pairs of siblings where they will not directly interact but will mostly interact via the mother. This provides her with a central location on the web. The mother has more power and controls everything of a daughter. It means that she gets lots of narcissistic supply from it because everybody is relating only to her and forgetting about her own needs.

5.8.6. Competition

It begins during early childhood and worsens through adolescence. Women may become alarmed when their daughters begin to mature. Competitiveness causes the mother to want her daughter to never reach higher than she has. Narcissistic mothers make it hard for their daughters to achieve. The mother is envious and jealous of her own daughter. It has a negative impact on the daughter. If the daughter is not completely co-dependent on the mother, she will have trust issues.

5.9 Do Daughters become narcissistic women

Narcissistic mothers may or may not produce narcissistic daughters. The chances are fifty-fifty. They can produce

- Co-dependent daughters.

- Borderlines (BPD).

This all is about survival and the victim. Every daughter internalizes the experience of a narcissistic mother in a very different way. Though the mother's affection and care are conditional, daughters adopt unsafe, harsh perceptions and being unlovable. These mothers set the daughters up for sadness, stress, self-worth, and association problems.

Feelings of denial at the age of puberty impact daughters to become narcissistic. They may tend to develop NPD due to exaggerated grandiosity, marginalization, breaking the limits, and blaming their daughter. Their integrity, confidence, and existence all need the approval of toxic mothers. These daughters are usually the golden child in the eyes of a mother.

While the scapegoat will decide on her own to give her mother a shut-up call to claim her own existence, she might have no or low contact to develop mentally, physically, and emotionally. They detach themselves from toxic mothers as they can no longer engulf the venom forcefully.

Hence one can say there is no hard and fast rule that narcissistic mothers produce narcissistic daughters.

5.10 Tolerating Toxic Mother

In certain terms, ill-willed women are permitted to rear children. Misguided ego-driven females who depend on their own impulses are empowered to become mothers to vulnerable, precious little daughters who are defenseless and taking all at face value when growing up.

Narcissistic mothers are deceptive and envious, leading them to raise their daughters to be miserable and actually wish them to hurt.

How do daughters secure their minds now that they are no longer free to be a helpless, trusting little girl?

1. Take a step out of isolation to build an understanding of the fact that the mother's illness brings.
2. Enable a childlike part of love and identify with a deeper reality.
3. Find oneself overflowing with fear for several reasons.
4. Understand that daughters are not willing to count on mothers who worshipped and utopian zed their existence.
5. Refuse to encourage the mother to continue to insist that daughters suffer for her, her desires, and wishes, which can never cease.
6. Understand what she's done and hurt experienced.
7. Intend on recovering and healing, so take this opportunity to develop solid resources (wellness routines, group friendships, etc.)
8. Develop limits; however, it is better to resist the mother.
9. Be boredom to mother as a narcissistic mother hates being boring
10. Set up connections that are worthy, and get people that care about.
11. Taking care of self is vital. Get up, read, paint, cook, make art, swim, hike, dance, take an exercise class, blog, and protect self
12. Forgiveness is the road to liberation and joy. It is a profound philosophy and needs a radical shift in how much daughters care about their mother and accept the forgiveness and rejoicing God has for us.

5.11 When Daughter of Narcissistic mother Marries

Daughters with manipulative mothers, as small children and adults, suffer badly. Most of them don't know that until years ago, their mother was a narcissist. They accepted the family story, what their mother taught them. Mother was the emphasis of the household. From everyone, including her husband and children, she still got what she needed. It's what we believe as we grow up in this kind of family. These girls learn to blend into the woodwork or become 24/7 servants of their mother, still accessible to them.

Any vain mother's daughters idealize them, remembering how beautiful they are. They want to imitate and become like their moms. The kind of affection that these ladies draw—they're still in the center of publicity and devotion. They assume it's special and handled like that. The little daughter is ready to take her mother's crumbs so long as she appears to be in touch with her. The father is also oppressed quite early and used to advocate wealth and reputation.

It is not shocking that when these girls grow up and start to pursue love mates, shallow men are disturbed by them. These charmers are masters of women. When they utter their lines, they are smart process performers who believe what they mean. This is their job, and they play it upside down. Many narcissists' daughters repeat the trend of intensely communicating with another narcissist, a mom. This is an implicit social phenomenon of repetition.

We revert to what we know, understood early in our lives, and became familiar. I've communicated with several girls who have repeated this cycle and woke up to see what they did—repeating the psychological trauma they had experienced as infants. All of these girls understand what they mean, experience the full impact of their psychological influence on them, hear about the narcissistic personality, and split up their narcissistic wife. They've agreed that they will do whatever they can to rebuild themselves and their families, as difficult as divorce can and is sometimes. They are now able for the first time to be physically and mentally safe. They take complete responsibility to lead their lives, use their own artistic talents, and guide their spiritual ambitions.

Chapter 6: Overcoming Hurtful Legacy and Reclaiming Life

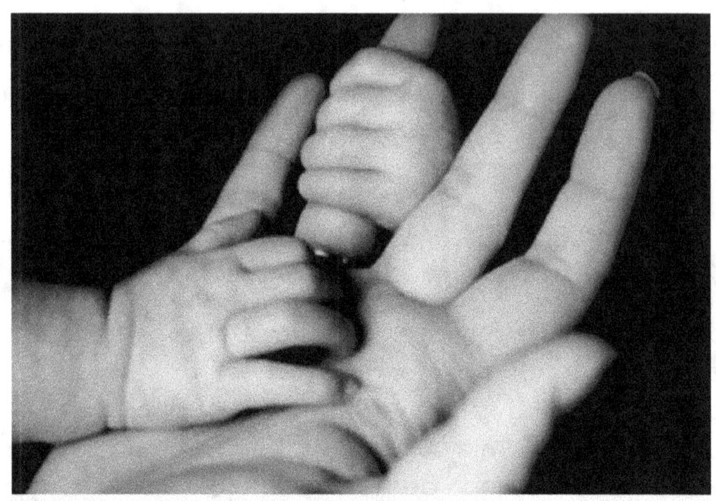

6.1. Healing from Narcissistic Abuse

In certain instances, victims of narcissistic violence are dismissed because they cannot leave the abusive arrangement. One would feel as though one was left with no anchor in the center of an ocean and no means of swimming back to shore. One doesn't understand why he abandoned himself, and one was able to do something right, but it wasn't good enough. The confusion is overwhelming. It is important to note that narcissists do not want to behave that way unless they suffer from a psychiatric illness. What has happened to the victim, then, is not your responsibility, nor former spouses.

He is unable to observe the inevitable development of a friendship because of his illness. There is no stage of interaction with a narcissist. They get bored and get overcome by depressive emotions once they have come down from their dopamine rush, and it is this that ushers in the process of devaluation. The narcissist would not sit back to plot this out; confirmation that it is a psychiatric condition is the reality that the bulk of narcissists behave in a common fashion.

The Three Stages in Narcissistic Violence

There are three phases of violence through narcissism. Victims characterize the feeling as being living on an emotional rollercoaster. As much as they believe it is important to hold their mate in a position of obedience, the narcissist may repeat the loop. The three processes contain the following:

1. *Idealize*

Narcissists threaten no one; they are searching for a mix of insecurity and prestige. For instance, an incredibly attractive woman who wants endless approval for a narcissist is the ideal companion.

Elegance provides them with respect, and insecurity suggests that his violence is extremely likely to be accepted, which ensures he makes a strong choice for narcissistic supply. Once they conclude that an entity is of worth, they follow them aggressively.

The narcissist would show off presents, praise, and assurances of the ideal partnership to their victim. The period of idealization is often recognized as the bashing of affection; this charismatic side of a narcissist makes it difficult to avoid.

2. *Devalue*

As the narcissist begins their depreciating assault in several situations, the target is indifferent to what is happening. At this point, they are so in love with the narcissist that they feel that nothing will possibly be wrong with him.

He cunningly masks insults as compliments; intuition will warn the person that everything is not quite right, but their perception has been clouded too much by the affection point; they sweep it under the carpet and behave as though all is okay.

The process of devaluation is quite disturbing when the narcissist continues to show a fractured personality in which they behave in general one way and in a personal one. They gradually initiate their assault and begin by attacking the peers and victim's family to separate them. The survivor becomes absolutely reliant upon the narcissist in this manner.

3. *Discard*

As a consequence of what they might get out of them, the narcissist can start finding others. The narcissist will discard their new companion until the victim loses its worth, and they are no longer having a supply.

The victim will undergo extreme deception known as gas lighting, projection, scapegoating, and blame-shifting during this phase. The period of discard is an intense variant of the phase of devaluation; the sugar coating has gone out of the window, and the true reign of chaos starts.

Perpetrators find this phase extremely tough to cope with, and the narcissist would criticize them for the abusive relationship breakup. They try every attempt to appease the narcissist so that they can experience the stage of affection again. However, the narcissist is prepared to step forward; there is little that can be done.

The 6 Recovery Steps Following Narcissistic Violence

Recovery from violence is a method, and on the path to rehabilitation, they can go through some challenging phases. There is no particular sequence for these processes, and they don't have to undergo any of them. But during an abusive partnership with a narcissist, these are the stages that are more likely to undergo.

1. *Denial*

The sense of denial after a manipulative partnership is not unusual. They are going to feel powerless and out of contact with reality. Since the victim has cherished their companion too much, the victim would not want to consider the person's failures to which the victim has committed your existence. For the victim's happiness, victims were relying on him but would feel better punishing for the violence than admitting that the victim fell in love with somebody who was willing to handle him in such a horrible way. This is not a deliberate choice; it is a truth in human psychology; following a stressful incident, many persons will feel this.

2. *Guilt Participation*

Narcissists carry out the tensions of their lives on their victims. On the person they are attacking, they project their defeats, setbacks, and wounds. Individuals are criticized for all that is bad, everything that goes wrong, for all the imperfections they find in themselves, and the things they do not correct.

People end up validating it after witnessing this each and every day and being conditioned to feel that the victim is at risk. Victims are always holding this responsibility as they quit the partnership because they feel bad that they were not successful enough to have him stay.

3. *Shame*

Shame has kept y victim locked in an unstable relationship; even despite breaking out of it, shame will hinder the victim from going on. In certain instances, a survivor will be pushed back into the embrace of their abusive abuser by the sense of guilt. The victim is going to experience guilt and humiliation because the victim feels deserving of the violence because it was his fault because he behaved in a manner that caused him to strike back.

In comparison, peers and relatives may be unconsciously disrespectful and ask victim demeaning queries. They subjectively glance at the case, and they don't know how to react to what the victim has gone through. They are posing these questions in their head, and they want to have a better understanding. Yet, they are accusing the victim in the head for encouraging the violence to continue, which further intensifies the sense of guilt.

4. Rage

The victim can look back until he has liberated himself from the bonds of an abusive association and wonder how the victim has ever been associated with such a person. For many factors, the victim would feel annoyed at himself; for not remembering what happened earlier, for the wasted time, for offering himself to such a cruel guy, for encouraging the beast to persuade the victim that his peers were not nice at all. The further victim analyzes what has occurred to him, and the more frustrated victim is likely to get.

5. Depression

Narcissistic violence is a part of emotional violence, and the partner would not put his hand on the victim in certain circumstances. But the lingering effects of violence of this nature will contribute to extreme depression. Life can feel heavy, and the victim will want to sleep away the agony on certain days; sleep will fail the victim on others.

Some days, the victim is not going to be able to feed; others are going to be living out of house and home. The victim will feel detached from the universe, but much of the time, victims feel nothing, only numbness. It is difficult to see the light as gloom prevails, and it becomes convenient to assume that this is the life that the victim would eternally live.

Depression occurs in waves because the minute victim believes he is feeling stronger; it's going to slip up on the victim and drive him back to his darkest days.

6. Recovery

Since passing through the steps of rehabilitation after narcissistic violence, redemption is a determination that only a victim can create. Starting to get to the stage that the victim really wants to get up, he is going to want to leave everything behind him, and he is going to start living again.

When victims are going to get here, there is no timetable since everybody is different. But the victim can either obtain clinical assistance at this stage, or the victim will continue to inform about how to get better and follow the advice.

6.2 Feelings after Narcissistic Abuse

They will undergo a lot of negative thoughts and feelings; sadly, following narcissistic violence, they are part of the phases of recovery. There are some of them that include:

6.2.1. Confusion

He made the victim feel so unique during the affection phase; no one in the universe could make him feel this way. The victim was his eye's apple, his eternal and unfailing devotion. He was going to get married one day and had a house full of girls.

During the depreciating phase of life, the victim realizes how cunningly the narcissist has exploited his emotions and trust, and this notion makes him stressed and confused. He remembers how narcissists were humiliated during the association phase in a humble tone.

6.2.2. Loneliness

If he had been in a relationship for a month or two years, his companion has been his life's passion, been together every single minute, and now gone. It is only normal that you would feel sad after the breakdown of a friendship/ relationship.

However, because of the intense peaks and downs, the narcissistic companion has brought to him, this isolation is heightened.

6.2.3. PTSD

The brutality that he witnessed was a sort of psychological assault, and he was traumatized by it. Trauma is described as an event that places his sense of safety or protection in danger. It is extremely difficult to be in a friendship or any association with someone suffering from a personality condition.

His feelings are unpredictable, and at all moments, he is in an elevated state of alert. This may cause post-traumatic stress disorder, including the following symptoms:

- Hallucinations,

- Inability to regulate the thoughts

- Suicidal thoughts/ fantasies

- Destructive coping techniques such as prescription medicine, misuse of narcotics or alcohol, eating disorders, and self-harm

- Trauma-related physical symptoms such as irritable bowel syndrome, tingling muscles, dizziness, chest pains, stomach aches, headaches

- Severe weariness and weakness

- The sensation of being numb/dissociative/disconnected/zoned out

- Shame/culpability

- Thinking for the worse in any case.

Not everyone who has recovered from an unhealthy manipulative association can get PTSD, but a significant diagnosis is post-traumatic stress disorder, and if he is having either of these concerns, it is important that he actively obtains therapeutic assistance.

Life will look very different now. He is not in an abusive relationship anymore but has to go through the healing process.

Healing is difficult, and it will be times when the pain will feel worse than the injury.

6.3 What to do After Abusive Association with Narcissist

It's not convenient to move forward. However, it is necessary. It requires a lot of emotional resources to repair the wounds that the victim has suffered, yet he will live a rewarding existence again if he has been willing. Here are some tips to start:

6.3.1. Stay alone

The terrible move he can do after stepping out of an unstable relationship is to get into a new one. He needs time to recover, continue and grow to respect himself again.

Stepping from one to another is a coping mechanism, a way to mask pain. Since he is already insecure, he faces another toxic partnership.

Staying alone is an essential part of the process of healing.

6.3.2. Be humble

Delete every link with that narcissist that is presents, photographs, text messages, and cards. No need for any reminders, whether good or bad, to throw them out, burn them or shred them. Go shopping, makeover, go on holiday.

Whatever it is, do it, and after all of the pain been through, it is necessary and deserves.

6.3.3. Learn to hear

Mates, family members, and partners would all believe they have the best cure for the victim. If the suggestion doesn't make them more relaxed, don't follow it, do what he thinks is right.

6.4 Keeping Narcissistic Mother in Life or Not

Many children want to confront or cut off their narcissistic mothers but to detach is the best in their interest. By emotionally and physically detaching from toxic mothers, it helps to get free from the destruction of narcissism or NPD. The child has the option or choice to turn his sad, lethargic, and stagnant life into happiness, self-growth, and discovery of true self. He will shift from hell to paradise. This choice makes him tension-free and relieved that he is no more under the control of a monster.

No contact

He may observe no contact or low contact with his narcissistic mother.

He may not answer her emails, calls, texts, invitations, etc., or not respond to her pleas for forgiveness and vows of change. No more believing in her lies and allowing no manipulation.

Low contact

But this becomes difficult when they are in a familial relationship, especially with a narcissistic mother. For this, he can observe low contact to protect himself from severe effects on his mental health. He may have an emotional detachment from her under the same roof. This makes him in charge of his feelings and judgments, can deal with different situations the way he feels best.

She may get irritated with this notion and gets fierce as she needs to survive with her destruction and toxicity. He shall be fully equipped to endure her tactics.

6.5 Strategies to Deal with Narcissistic Mother

Following are the strategies to heal the damage caused due to over-caring or ignoring the attitude of a narcissistic mother

6.5.1. Avoid reaction

Narcissistic mothers often wait for a response to flee from the blame and put the child's responsibility. They use exploitative techniques to make an emotional trap. Sometimes they will intentionally push their "weak points" to incite a child to anger. After a break, they will play the victim's happy role and blame a child that he overreacted. When growing up under her care, one had to deal with a mother. The negative effects of narcissistic mothers on their offspring can be severe, and children may be conditioned to do whatever they can to keep their mothers happy.

By telling her not to reply, one is telling her that what she's doing is fine, and one will continue to take the abuse. Children do care about their mom and want to protect her. But stand up to her and resist, don't let her have her way all the time. She may attempt to get even with the child but stand strong.

6.5.2. To empathize

Toxic mothers have a weak, traumatic, and brutal inner world. They do not even understand their own psyche. Their reason for being discontent makes them not seeing how their actions are. A child, for his own tranquility, must develop a compassionate strategy.

6.5.3. To have no arguments

Disagreeing with narcissistic mothers is useless as they never consider anyone else's standpoint. They will support their arguments with facts and will twist a child's words. They will discover new ways to dodge answerability and will not let a child call them a liar. The more a child argues and imposes his point of view, the more he gets stuck in.

6.5.4. Maintaining Confident position

Children raised by narcissistic mothers often have subconscious conditioning. To seek mother's approval, authenticity, and love. These children usually lack an objective approach. If a child understands this, it will be easier to give in his need for his mother to consent with him and reiterate his point of view.

6.5.5. Impersonal

A child must detach himself from the behavior of his narcissistic mother. This will help to practice distancing emotional attachment. Whatever she is projecting on a child originates from her inner turmoil.

6.5.6. Take time

A narcissistic mother has a lot of desires and dreams for her children. They are not only indebted for her admiration but to do everything she desires. There are many gratification and undertakings a mother will shower upon her children. If a child agrees to please her (at first impulse), he might have to tolerate bitterness in the long run. So, don't say "yes" to her unless he means it.

6.5.7. Self-confidence

No matter how talented and brilliant a child is, but developing with a narcissistic mother meant living in hell. It may not be easy to be applauded with his accomplishments because a child has internalized his mother's voice. Hence a child must accept the way he is. Also, cognitive behavior treatment helps in pointing out "faulty programming" and enables the brain to think again in a different way. This will enhance self-confidence and the ability to live a courageous life.

6.5.8. Set limits

A narcissistic mother manipulates to devalue a child. A child might be subjected to abuse regularly, and this should not be disregarded or endured. This happens when an adult sets the conditions of the agreement to live with a narcissistic mother, and what will happen if the narcissist acts against this agreement.

It sounds complicated but is really simple. Be very definite and explicit about the behavior that a child will not endure. This way, a person is putting the blame on her. It is on her if she loses, and a child leaves. It is difficult to establish boundaries with a narcissistic mother, but it is still possible. Have off-limits and enforce that rule, no matter how much she whines.

If parents are not around, then establishing a certain day and/or time, they can come over. If she comes after those times, make it clear that she will not be allowed in. If she comes in, she'll be waiting outside. Give this a shot to maximize effectiveness.

The most common method is to say nothing, but others may share more or less. She needs to know that adults are separate from her and that they have privacy.

6.5.9. Identify Narcissistic Behaviors in adults

As a result of having narcissistic mothers throughout their lives, some kids pick up some unhealthy narcissistic behaviors. Many of these things can have a negative effect on a kid's life and other relationships. To check for Narcissistic Traits, it might be a good idea to step back and see how the mother has influenced adults.

6.5.10. Self-care

Healthy methods in self-care may aid in healing. Self-care is one's mental and physical needs.

It includes:

- Get ample sleep.

- Rest when depressed.

- Set the time for games.

- In touch with peers.

- Develop coping skills to handle depression.

- Consuming healthy meals.

- Exercising daily.

- Taking care of physical needs will assist with mental pain.

6.5.11. Treatment

Adults of narcissistic mothers need treatment and counseling if narcissistic behaviors/traits are found in them. Therapy or counseling is always a good idea. People who aren't currently struggling with mental health issues should speak with a professional. Adults will have a safe space to speak about their issues with their parents. They can help understand how to live with a narcissistic mother and how to fix co-narcissistic behaviors.

If looking for how to confront a narcissistic mother, these professionals can help. Not only do they have the knowledge to treat people with NPD, but they also have experience dealing with people with similar issues.

If adults developed mental health issues, a therapist could also help walk healthy ways to cope. If needed, they can refer a psychiatrist to help diagnose the problem and recommend the appropriate treatment.

To treat mental health issues, adults need medications that make it easier to deal with their narcissistic mothers.

6.6 How does recovery work?

Children who come from narcissists need to go through the following five stages. Reverting back and forth between these stages may be common.

6.6.1. Acceptance

Accepting that a narcissistic mother is difficult to be around for a child is a difficult step for recovery. It is difficult for every child to digest that their mother does not like them unconditionally, shows no emotions, and only considers their own existence. The only solution to this is not comparing one's mothers with others.

6.6.2. Denial

This treatment allows children to shield themselves. Children need their mother's care and sympathy. When a child gets mature, he needs to ignore the mistakes and errors of his mother and endure the fact she is not perfect.

6.6.3. Hope

When one is a toddler, he struggles to win his narcissistic mother's love, but all in vain. A child never creates a dispute with his mother, so do what she wants him to do. He hopes that his mother will change and his desire will come true. One should ignore this hope and keep a positive vibe to amuse a narcissistic mother.

6.6.4. Angel

The children of narcissistic mothers usually have anger issues as sentimental needs are not fulfilled. Suppressing anger can lead to disruptive behavior. If a child allows himself to be annoyed and talks to someone confidant who understands his feelings. This will make him better.

6.6.5. Depression

Depression may occur. Children of narcissists feel gloomy and useless because they realize they will never have a normal parent-child relationship and that they will never be loved the way they wanted to be. Depression is common when experiencing such a dramatic change. Try to drag himself out of it.

6.7 Golden child and scapegoat- Survival versus Victim

Scapegoat syndrome

Early childhood deprivation and sensitivity to physical and sexual violence will, over time, lead to suffering from psychiatric disorders. While studies show that traumatic childhood conditions such as tension, violence, and brutality sometimes contribute to poor mental wellbeing. Researchers showed that those who endured childhood abuse were at greater risk of suffering overall fitness, along with a serious rate of heart failure. The researchers come to the conclusion that "the consequences of past abuse endure for an entire life."

When someone considered a scapegoat comes to the notice, he also suffers from the disorder. Several people have named this "scapegoat child syndrome." The expression is not entirely true, though, since this isn't a formal word like the sense that psychiatric conditions are. There are a number of longer-term impacts that the scapegoated kid might encounter.

- Trust issues.

- Thinking negatively of them and labeled as losers.

- People who do not have a healthy family life suffer from discomfort that may contribute to a feeling of loss of connection.

- Sometimes it does harm to their sense of self.

- These individuals may be attracted to friends and partners that are dominant or narcissistic.

Golden child syndrome

The detrimental consequences of becoming the golden child named golden child syndrome. It has the following impact on the hero of a narcissistic mother

- ***They cannot try to understand that mistakes and shortcomings are OK.*** One ought to be worthy of making errors in order to succeed in life. The gold children have to understand that they'll be forgiven for all of their errors. They also have to know that people who support us will always love us if we screw up. This is regarded as "psychological safety." Yet, they also get their errors and failures pushed under the carpet by the golden boy. So, they might get frightened by failure in the future.

- ***The sense of being vulnerable.*** When they are granted high praise and informed, they are exceptional, gifted, creative, and wise, the praise is typically focused on everything that they've achieved. However, without them having achieved anything to merit it, the narcissist shows certain praise on the golden boy. This is called overvaluation. The dilemma here is that this recognition is desired for the golden kid, but they don't realize that they merit it. Feeling undeserving will make people feel uncertain when they have no basis in understanding whether the recognition will arrive in the future.

- ***Do not seem to have power.*** Getting a golden kid as a sibling comes with expectations—including catering to the selfish parent's needs. Their parents gave them extended privileges and may not allow them to be themselves. Because of this, it may be difficult for individuals with this disorder to establish their own identities.

- ***Terrified***. Know that they are indeed a kid at heart. The more authoritarian parent assigned this position to them, and a child goes along with it since a child may not have the ability to think differently. However, as they grow older, when realizing that they were complicit in the exploitation of the scapegoat kid, they develop great remorse.

In a narcissistic mother's family, one child is the Golden Child, and one or more is the Scapegoat. The Golden Child is the superb and the most amazing child, at least in the eyes of the Narcissistic Mother. Narcissistic mothers may end up engulfing the Golden Child. He may nurture well but with no self-worth. He is likely to remain as a permanent victim of the narcissist or, if he does ever manage to break free, that process will be more painful than it was for the Scapegoat. The scapegoat is self-reliant. He's the one who seeks answers and realizes narcissism. He still finds it hard to swallow.

Given the propensity of golden children to have a close connection with their parents, it is not irrational to believe that a partnership will be tense between the golden child and the scapegoat.

In some instances, they will participate in the violence aimed towards the scapegoat. Likewise, the narcissistic parent would not encourage the partnership to ever take shape, something that will prevent a stable relationship from even being established. Of course, they would definitely foster competition and aggression among their hostages, utilizing triangulation as a means of manipulating them.

While the scapegoat is considered the stigma to the family, this leads to a rivalry between children, which befit the narcissistic mother. It gives her lots of opportunities to employ manipulative tactics.

The Scapegoat is also named the Identified Patient. All the ills of the family are projected onto him. It's not surprising if maltreated and humiliated and treated with injustice and the whole life, and he might have problems like eating disorders, addiction, anger management issues, or depression, etc. And this magnifies the slogan that he is the bad and wrong one. The scapegoat even believes he is the "bone of content" child. The toxic mothers might consider him mentally upset and take him to get fixed through therapy. The scapegoat is in a bad situation. It is rarely a serious enough problem to warrant social services.

6.8 Tips for Survival of Narcissistic mothers

6.8.1. Compassion is still the law

They have done an exceptional job of navigating very demanding puberty. Instead of giving loving encouragement, they have often been ridiculed and humiliated. They received sympathy, but they didn't get it. To be the perfect mother or father they've never had, they have to learn how to do it. As survivors, they are always so hard on themselves. If they feel stressed and depressed, leave all of that and be sweet to themselves. They are permitted to feel anxious and nervous. Imagine trying to comfort the most loving mother. Therefore, it is important to recognize that once they have genuine kindness and affection for themselves, one does not have the capacity to freely give empathy or intimacy to others.

6.8.2. Pardon Oneself

They have never been prompted to make mistakes. When they make an error, they are motivated by a loving mother and made to benefit from it. If this lesson were to expand, think of where they will be now! Without pounding over it, they should switch from one mistake to another, but instead tell to say to Self: Yeah, it's all right, I'm a human being. They trusted her for a long time if they had a selfish mum, but they might still be unsure of what a healthy relationship looks like. It takes time to learn to respect oneself and to strive to meet people who support one another and express true love. Forgive oneself because it is still a vital phase in the journey to find real self and value all their emotions to trust the wrong people in the manner they believe.

6.8.3. Have inner uncertainty

Everyone also has inner chaos too. It is a part of human life on this earth. One does not and does not assume that they are on top and that all works out all the time! Perhaps because she was so smart and right, she felt compelled to beat them down and never gave them credit for brilliant concepts; Toxic Mother may have made them feel this way. So, while they were not on top and eventually felt uncertain over some unexplained incident in their lives, they may have taken this opportunity to point out that as well. For them, this was really overwhelming and painful, which only made them tougher on themselves. It's too unhealthy to aspire for flawlessness. All the years they have lost, feeling unworthy of acceptance and like they were not nice enough at any time, they have to grieve.

6.8.4. Remorse

Humiliation and distrust are thoughts and feelings from elsewhere that can be dismissed. It is difficult to stop the "inner critic" because it feels like "self" sending them these negative thoughts because they assume it might be true. These signals and thoughts, though, are not from the real self. They are false beliefs they have internalized by surviving their narcissistic mum!

6.8.5. Speaking out and seeking support

It helps to understand the root of this disturbing loop if the project bursts of anger and desperation to loved ones and is confused over why this is happening. This is termed "transference" of inner child sadness, which is a really necessary and critical part of the mechanism of healing.

6.9 Tips for the victim of Narcissistic Mothers

6.9.1. Don't name her narcissist

That's often enticing, but it's usually gone horribly wrong, making matters worse. Typically labeling somebody, a narcissist is supposed to make them pause and worry about their harm. Yet individuals with a narcissistic personality disorder cannot focus on their own actions and become concerned with showing the one with an issue. They are far better than victims. They learn knowledge from people's reviews, no matter how beneficial or strong it may be. Only ignore it. Victims won't give them insight into themselves. And they can potentially exacerbate the partnership.

6.9.2. No Arguments

It does not serve to disagree with them for the same reason. They won't get ideas from the reviews. And they needn't protect themselves, so it's not about them. It's just their attitude and lack of communication skills. They prefer to view it all-or-nothing, and then the blame is all theirs and all the victimhood. They can't change it. They always see themselves as victims-in-life, viewed very harshly by those around them, without understanding their own role of the dilemma-which could be the biggest part of the problem. Arguing just places them in their brain's emotional sections, where they change to strong protective gear.

6.9.3. Focus on choices

Mom of selfish personalities often mourns their everyday lives. She demands that people misperceive her without due thought. She doesn't see how her own behaviors influence how people avoid or respond to her. It also helps understand the victim's choices. A narcissist can drain psychologically, triggering undue self-criticism. They can prefer to disregard them, shorten the time, or take someone else with them when they're around. Even understanding they have choices makes things less daunting. Even she may select constraints.

6.9.4. Set Limits

And though victims can't control their narcissistic mother's acts, they can regulate theirs. Instead of seeking to make her happier, see how the victim may adjust. One of the first forms of looking is how their narcissism may be tolerated or supported. By pursuing the most love and loyalty, criticizing others (even parents), undermining the family's rules, and manipulating decision-making, a deceptive sibling or child steadily gains power in many cultures. The victim doesn't need to cooperate. For their actions against others, she may lack some interest or act towards the perpetrator as well.

6.10. Healing from Narcissistic Mothers Require Self-care

Narcissistic moms are widespread today. Manipulative individuals currently surround us, and culture naturally embraces and honors them. Many are high and socially smooth to blend seamlessly into our obsessed world portrait.

Narcissistic mothers can't love them. Asked to become narcissists? No. Causes their children psychological harm? Yes. The narcissistic mother's psychodynamics with her child is very complicated yet simple. There's no way to be our true self because we have a mother that is physically and mentally inaccessible, who accuses kids of anything they do or don't do, and who continually projects her venom on us. The intense fear and anxiety and feelings of inadequacy and rootlessness induced by these mothers are colossal. These kids never had a real home where they could find warmth, relaxation, approval, love, independence, and psychological and emotional protection.

Home is a battle zone–the battles continue behind locked doors. Narcissistic mothers are intensely secretive; making sure their wonderfully built appearance remains flawless in the outside world. They intentionally develop connections with friends and colleagues and other family members to see them through the best light—as nice, kind, considerate people. Just a couple in a household or peer community isn't tricked. Sometimes these people stay silent and don't expose the facts because they're really frightened by the manipulative personality's power. They opt not to wave or talk.

Adult manipulative mother children thrive; however, they also endured terribly and in length. Some receive relief through psychotherapy, counseling, engaging through body/mind link to learn how to relax the nervous system that has been suffering or escaping for most of their life.

One critical part of recovery from the psychological wound of getting a manipulative mother is to understand that they have to be very cautious eventually. They pursue this practice steadily, beginning with the fundamentals. Next, realize they have the right to have some genuine peace in their lives; they deserve to have some buddies they trust and depend on.

One of the greatest lessons is how to avoid criticizing self endlessly. Switch aside from the inner critique placed from infancy. Practicing a method of relaxing the mind is really effective here. Practice can take several forms: brief led meditations on cd or tube that can be useful to them individually. Practicing soft hatha yoga where they relax through the nose and concentrate on each posture at the moment is a way to move to the parasympathetic, quiet nervous system. Having the sleep they need and deserve triggers a detox schedule. Nourishing the body with foods that build resilience, endurance and stabilize their system is important.

Flowing the imaginative juices is one of the strongest tonics for a selfish mother's healers. So many forms they might dream about manifesting their imagination. Start writing these down immediately without thought and they'll be shocked at the brilliant ideas pouring from them.

Know they're entitled to recovery. It's the self-discovery path to inner harmony and perfection. This method is forever worth any move. Start this moment, watch the mechanism develop. Be proud of their lovely girl.

Conclusion

This book gives an insight into narcissism, narcissistic mothers, their traits, and tactics, which have long-lasting divesting effects from childhood to adulthood. Though a mother is everything in an individual's life, sometimes they do have a "hidden monster" in them, which undermines the self-respect, needs, desires, dreams, and passion of a child.

During adolescence, when one configures that a mother is suffering from narcissism, an adult needs to adopt strategies to deal with such toxic mothers. This will lessen the consequences of side-effects on an adults' physical, emotional and mental health.